10 X 10
LOCKDOWN

10 X 10 LOCKDOWN

Ten creative responses of ten women
to the Coronavirus pandemic lockdown

Compiled by
Penny Perrett

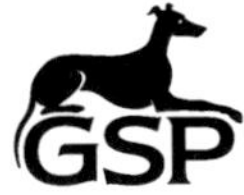

10 x 10 Lockdown
Compiled by Penny Perrett

Published by Greyhound Self-Publishing, 2020
Malvern, Worcestershire, United Kingdom.

Designed by Sue Haslam

Printed and bound by Aspect Design
89 Newtown Road, Malvern, Worcs. WR14 1PD
United Kingdom
Tel: 01684 561567
E-mail: allan@aspect-design.net
Website: www.aspect-design.net

A copy of this book has been deposited with the British Library Board

ISBN 978-1-909219-72-4

Contents

To Live

as if to wrench some joy from every day,
to wade through washing up, achieve a smile;
to hang the picture frame another way,
to drive the family car another mile,
to nearly find your niche, the easy buck,
to lift your head above the parapet,
to honour your sacred dead, to give a fuck,
your lines and wrinkles deeper, deeper set.

To love as if, to give as if, to dance
as if your world does not depend on chance,
to fashion beauty underneath the tatters,
to find the spotlight, take the final bow
as if, within the unrelenting now,
as if your joy could last, as if it matters.

Amanda Bonnick

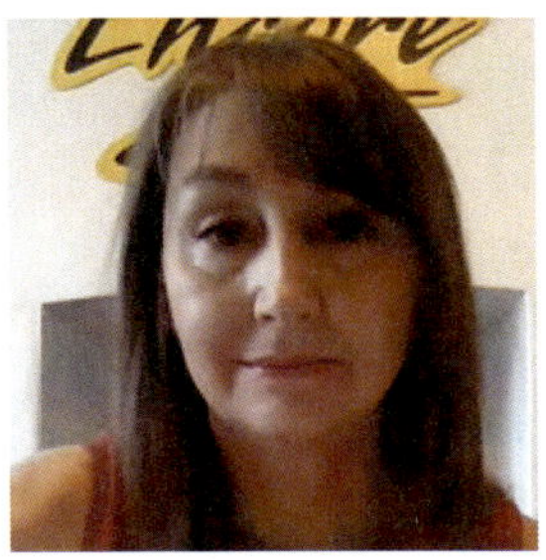

***Amanda Bonnick** is a Worcester writer and is currently Poet in Residence for Worcester Cathedral (2019/20). She is also a producer, director and actor with Melting Pot Theatre Company. She has co-hosted the Word and Sound open mic event and has performed her poetry at Parole Parlate, SpeakEasy, Licensed to Rhyme, and Stirchley Speaks spoken word events. She has recently published her poetry pamphlet 'Pick Your Own' with Worcester's Black Pear Press and her work has appeared in anthologies 'Voices of 1919' (by Mike Alma), 'Ripples' by Jackie Summer, and several small presses (Envoi, Fire, Critical Survey, Agenda).She is currently writing her third novel in a children's fiction series.*

10 X 10 LOCKDOWN

10 x 10 Lockdown started as a way to acknowledge my brilliantly creative women friends. During lockdown, established artists had time to spend on new ideas and at the same time, people who had not considered themselves to be artists discovered paint, pencil, camera and words to express fears and thoughts as lockdown was introduced in March 2020. Often these were shared on Facebook and it was when I was enjoying looking at these that I came up with the idea of pulling them together into a book.

So, I decided to ask ten women to share ten ideas that they had created over ten days between March and June 2020. The interim project was called 10 cubed. Sue Haslam and I had worked together for Worcestershire Arts Education and then later on a project for Worcester Foodbank and I knew she would be just the person to put our ideas into a book format. She is a visual artist in her own right and we agreed to compile the work together. We decided we wanted to have something to hold rather than simply have a product that was only on-line: a memory to reflect on ourselves and a memory for our children and grandchildren to look at in years to come.

During lockdown, we all shared a new way of looking at our world, the beauty of calm and the sound of birdsong. At the same time, those of us living alone found settling to anything difficult and missed the comfort of friends and family. We needed to find new ways of distracting ourselves from watching too much news, even though watching news was addictive.

The arts have always been a way to reflect on our world and lockdown has offered opportunities and time to discover new ways of exploring our environment with beauty and humour.

The outcome is here to hold and flick through.

Penny Perrett

Diamonds on the Soles of Her Shoes

Anne Greer

I have always loved colour. For many years I worked as a graphic designer, and then as a partner with NHS hospitals, trying to get good colours into healthcare settings. When I retired, I turned my professional interest into something more personal: quilting. My Swedish great-grandmother and grandmother were both quilters. I have simply picked up the fabric and followed them.

I think I have made more than fifty quilts over the last ten years – small and large, most of which are now covering family and friends, all over Worcestershire and well beyond. My grandchildren probably have too many.

'Colour and comfort' - that's how I think of quilting. During the lockdown period I decided to make a quilt that would help me remember this muted time. I used batik fabrics from my fabric stash. It's a very simple design: two joined triangles make each square, and the squares are sewn together to make the quilt top. I always line my quilts with fleece, because that makes them super soft, and washable, too.

I often listen to the radio while I'm quilting, but this quilt was made mostly to the sound of Paul Simon's 'Graceland' album. When I look at it in the future, I'll be humming, 'Diamonds on the soles of her shoes...'

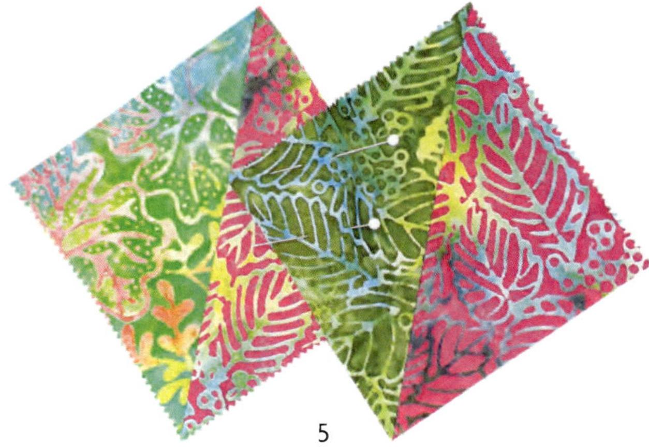

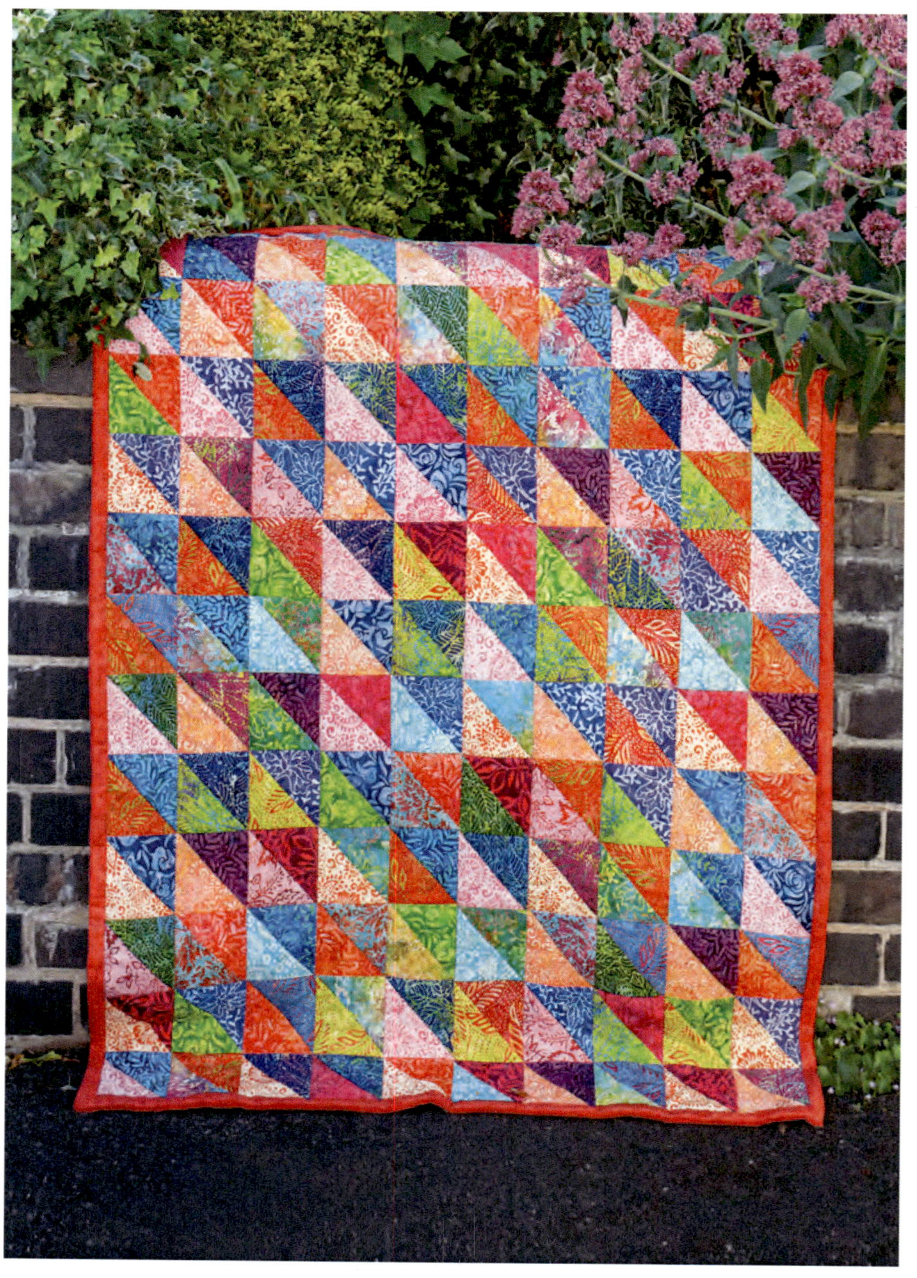

Haiku Renshi

Anne Greer and Sara Hayward

Anne Greer and Sara Hayward started a haiku renshi* in January 2020 – long before the words 'coronavirus', 'lockdown' and 'social distancing' were part of our common vocabulary.

"The idea was simple: that we would write a haiku (the Japanese form where three lines in a 5-7-5 syllable pattern constitute the poem) each in turn, week after week, and see where it led us. The last word of one poem would become the first word of the next poem, and we would pass the haiku between us, like a linked and growing chain.

We decided that Sunday was a good day for the exchange, by email, and found that we both eagerly looked forward to reading what the other had written. Hurry up Sunday!

We hope that we'll be able to complete an entire year's cycle: fifty-two haiku (yes, that's the plural) that will suggest the rhythm through the seasons, seen through our particular lenses.

There aren't any 'rules' other than the syllabic construction, and the challenge of using the word we are 'given' to begin the next haiku. As it happens, we both seem to avoid direct reference to events, although by keeping our attention on the natural world: the floods in February and our own perceptions of the encompassing pandemic came through in subtle ways.

For this 10 x 10 project, we've selected ten haiku – five by Anne, five by Sara, in turn-about fashion – that reflect ten weeks during this most curious time."

** 'renshi' refers to linked, collaborative poems*

SHINE OF SHARP RAINDROPS

DIAMONDS HURLED ON THE RIVER

FAST WATERS RISING

RISING WATERS FLOOD

FRUIT OF THE VINE A RESCUE

DROWNING OUR SORROWS

SORROWS, DROWNED, VANISH

MOMENTARILY BEFORE

SURFACING DOWNSTREAM

DOWNSTREAM AN OCEAN

DRAWS A FALLEN BRANCH – BROKEN

FROM JOURNEY UPSTREAM

UPSTREAM A HERON

REPAIRS LAST YEAR'S NEST AS SPRING

STIRS IN THE REED BED

BED OF PRIMROSES

MOSSY MATTRESS A CUSHION

SOOTHING SPRING HAS SPRUNG

SPRUNG FROM THE DARK SOIL

A ROGUE IRIS STRETCHES WHILE

REACHING FOR THE SUN

SUN A SPECTACLE

AS SHADOWS FALL A WELCOME

LENS AMIDST DARKNESS

DARKNESS LIFTS THE EDGE

OF NIGHT'S COVER REVEALING

DAWN'S SLENDER RIBBON

RIBBON OF SEEDLINGS

EMERGE FROM CRUMBLY DARK SOIL

BLINKING IN SUNSHINE

Me and My Cat Bob

by Jane Beesley

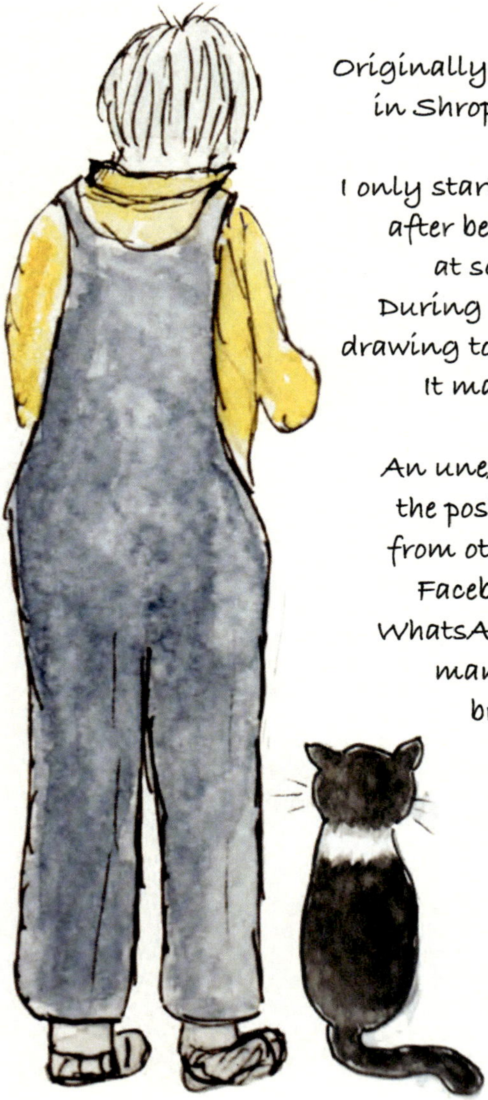

Originally from Yorkshire I now live in Shropshire with my cat Bob.

I only started drawing in February, after being told 'not to bother' at school 50 years ago. During lockdown I have found drawing to be completely absorbing. It makes my heart sing.

An unexpected bonus has been the positive feedback I've had from others. Posting daily on Facebook, Instagram and WhatsApp, they have rekindled many friendships and brought new ones.

My various series featuring Bob are my diary of this time.

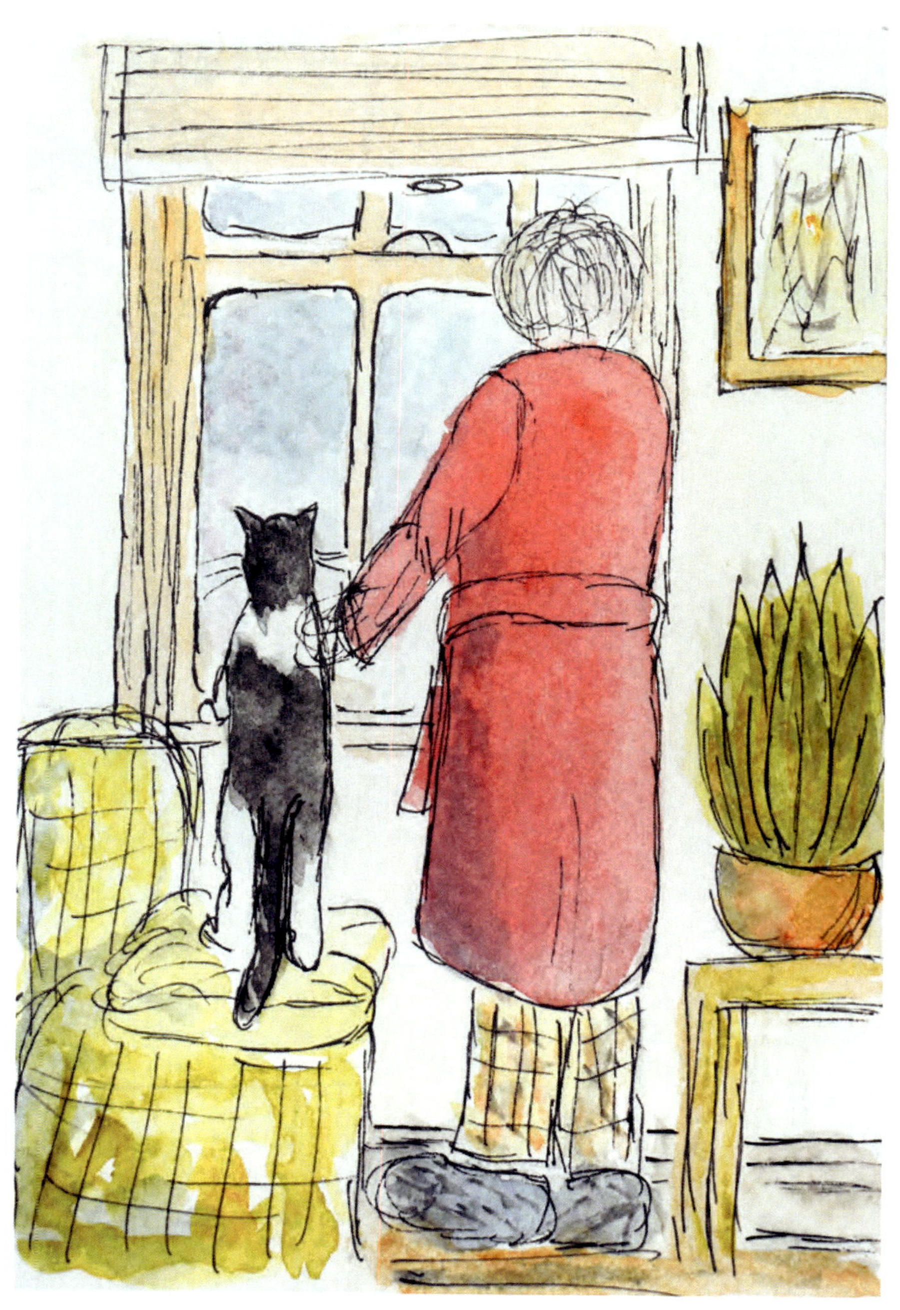

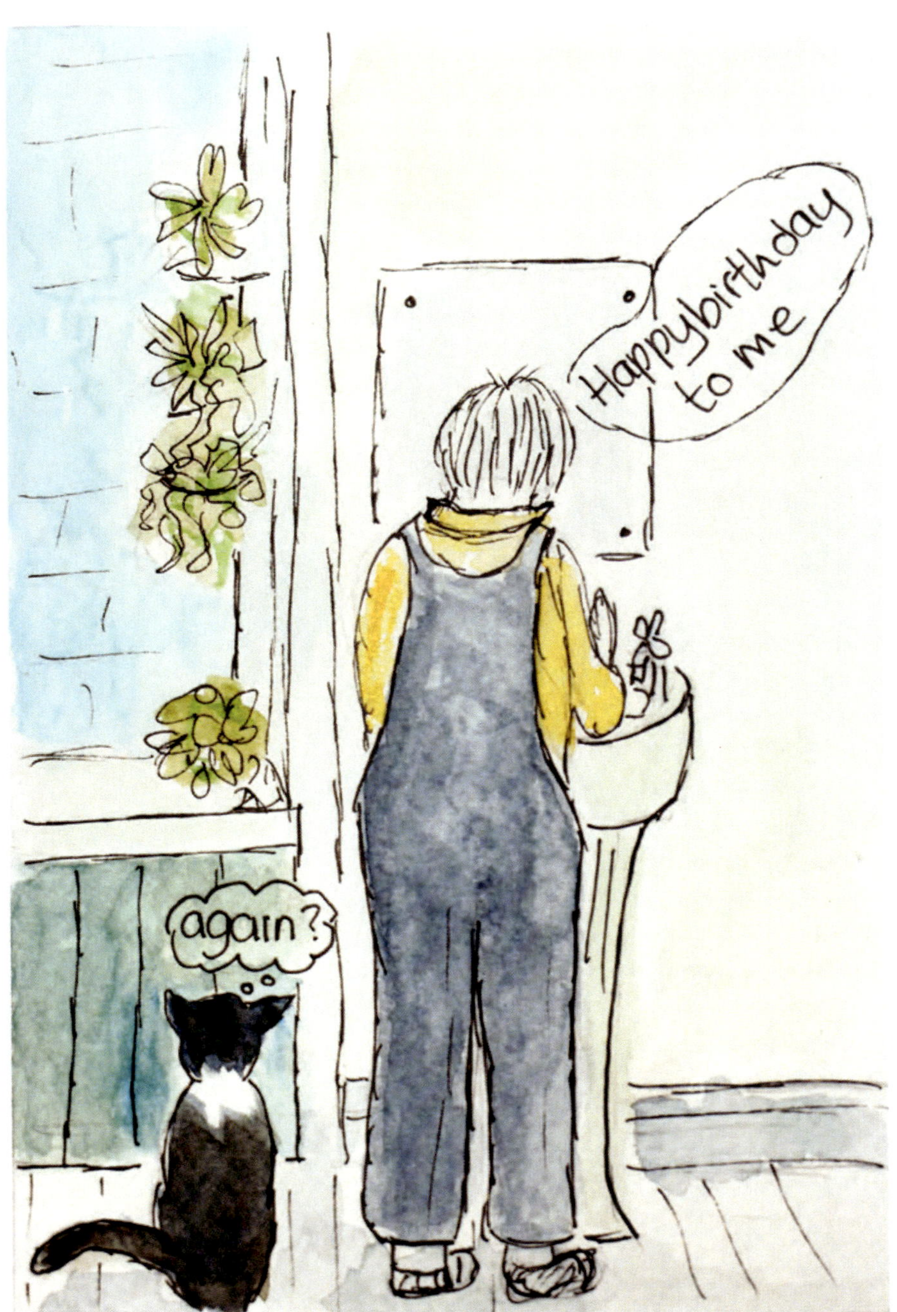
Happybirthday
to me
again?

Dear Bob... No 8

If I wear a mask how will people know how I'm feeling?

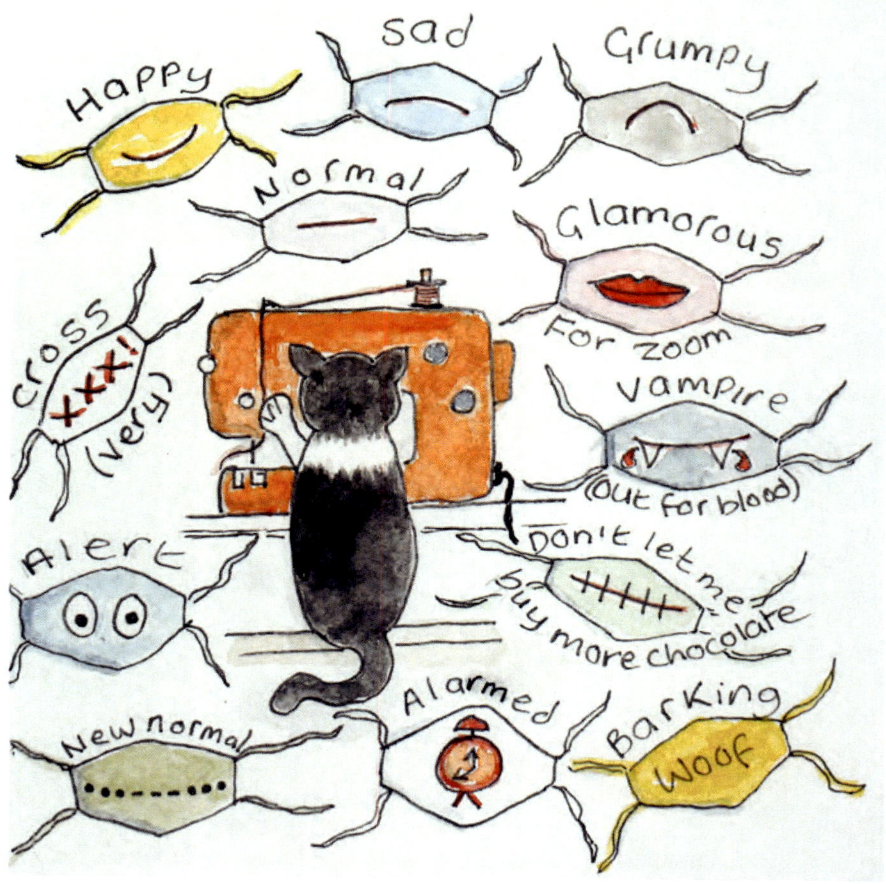

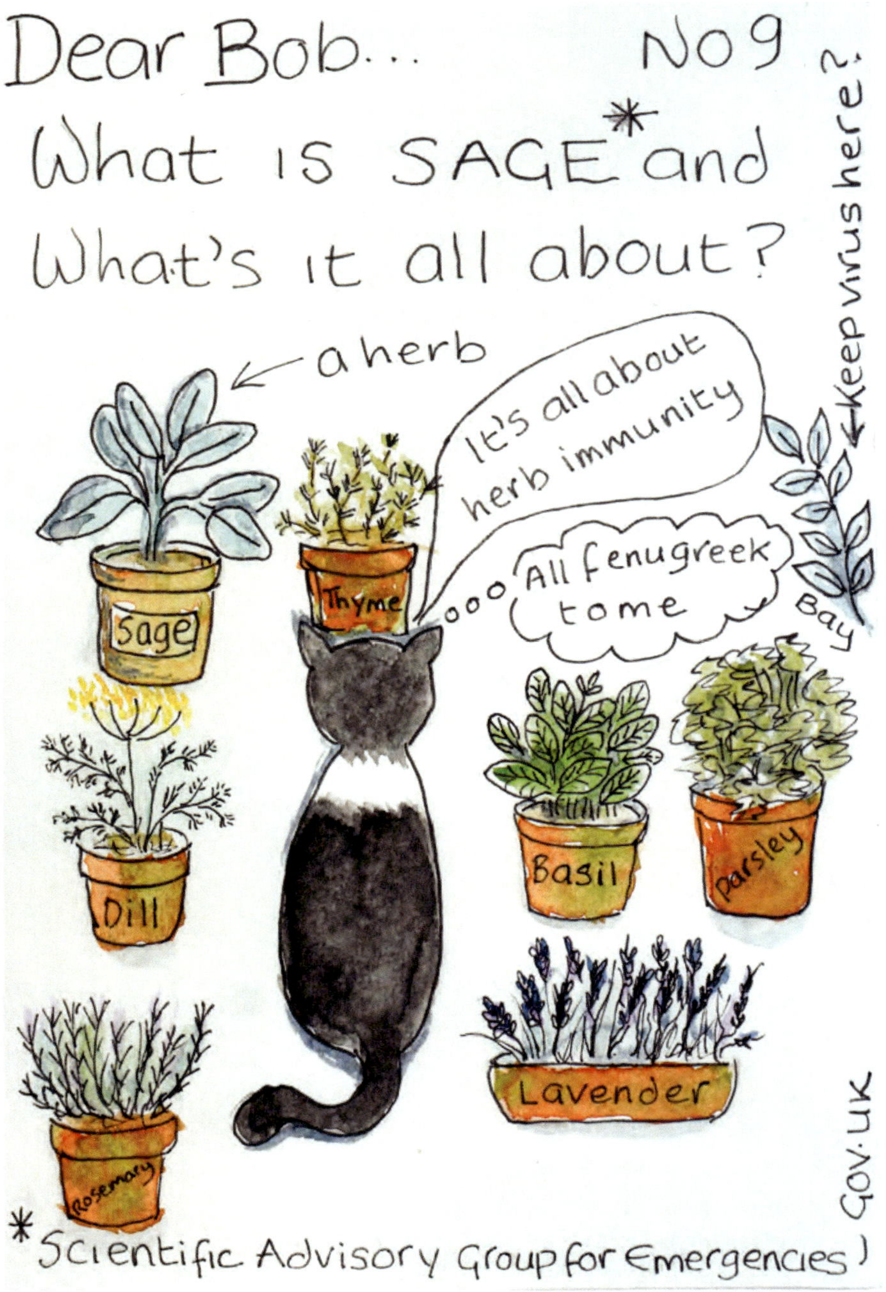

Dear Bob... No 9

What is SAGE* and What's it all about?

a herb

It's all about herb immunity

ooo All fenugreek to me

Keep virus here?

Sage

Thyme

Bay

Dill

Basil

Parsley

Rosemary

Lavender

GOV.UK

*Scientific Advisory Group for Emergencies)

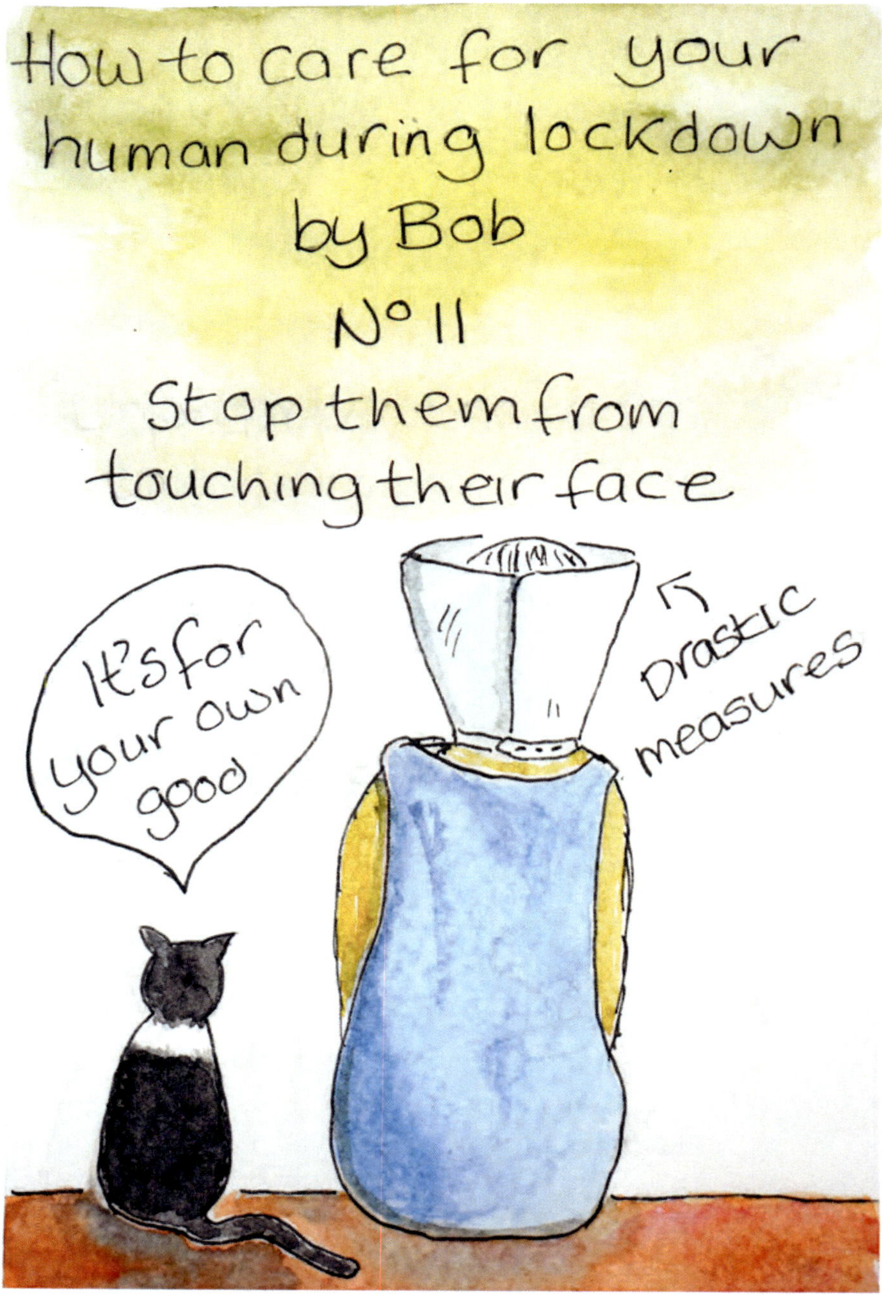

How to care for your human during lockdown
by Bob
N° 11
Stop them from touching their face

It's for your own good

Drastic measures

Dear Bob... Nº 12

Nevermind what day, month, year it is, What's the time?

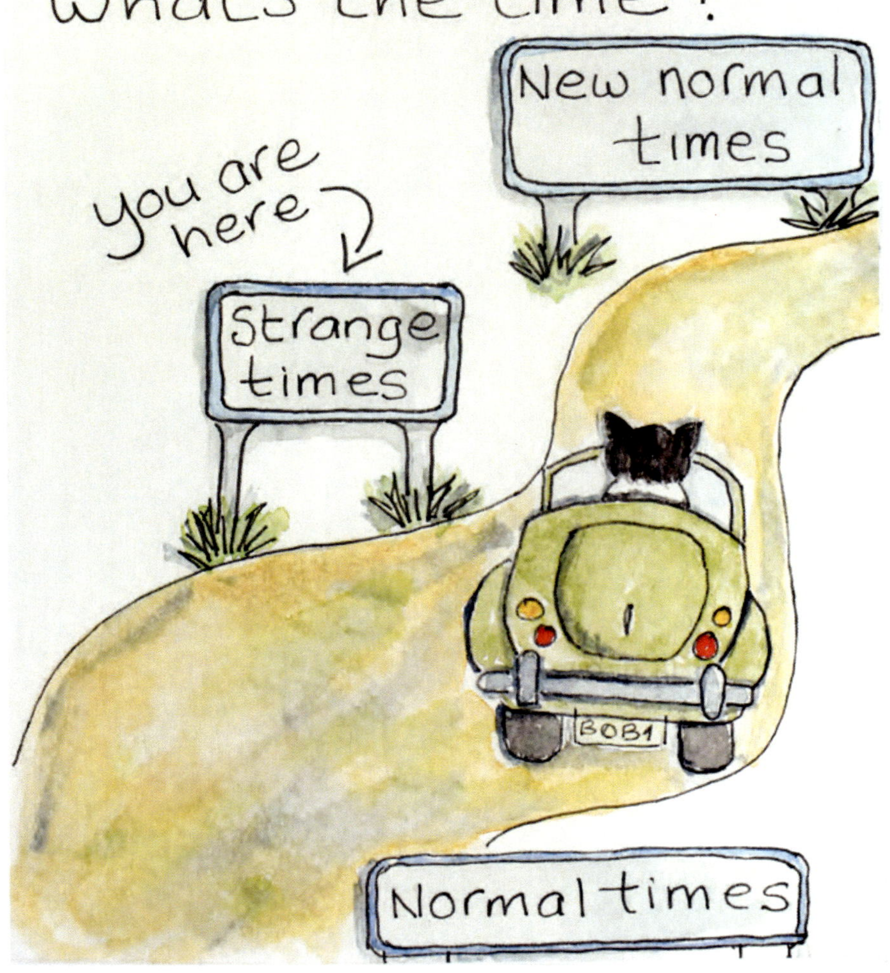

How to care for your human during lockdown by Bob

No 17
Knowing what day it is

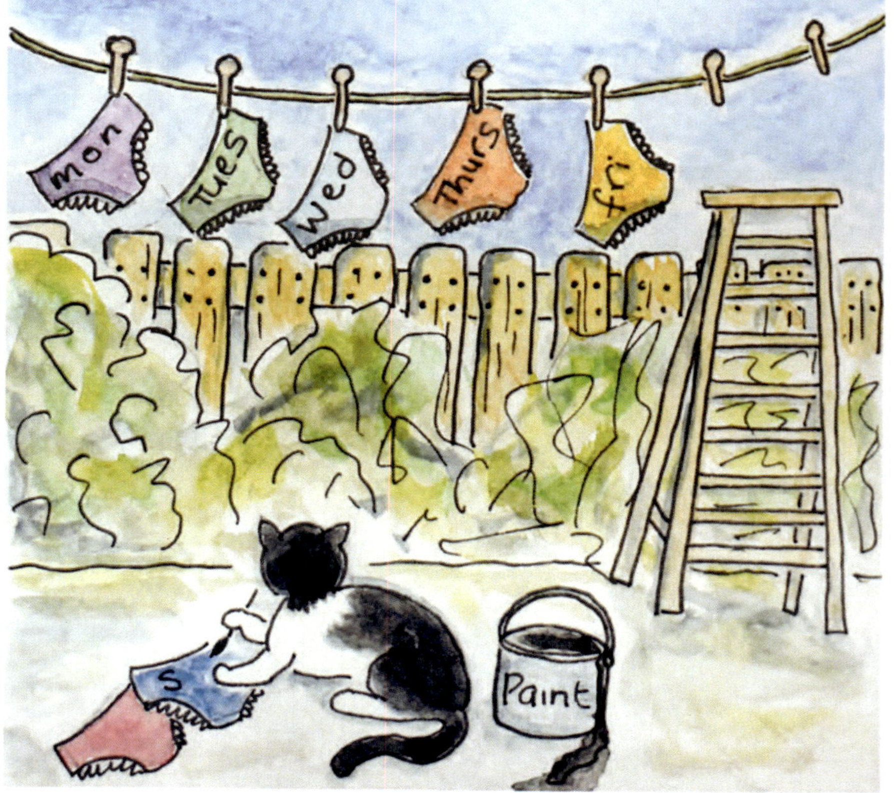

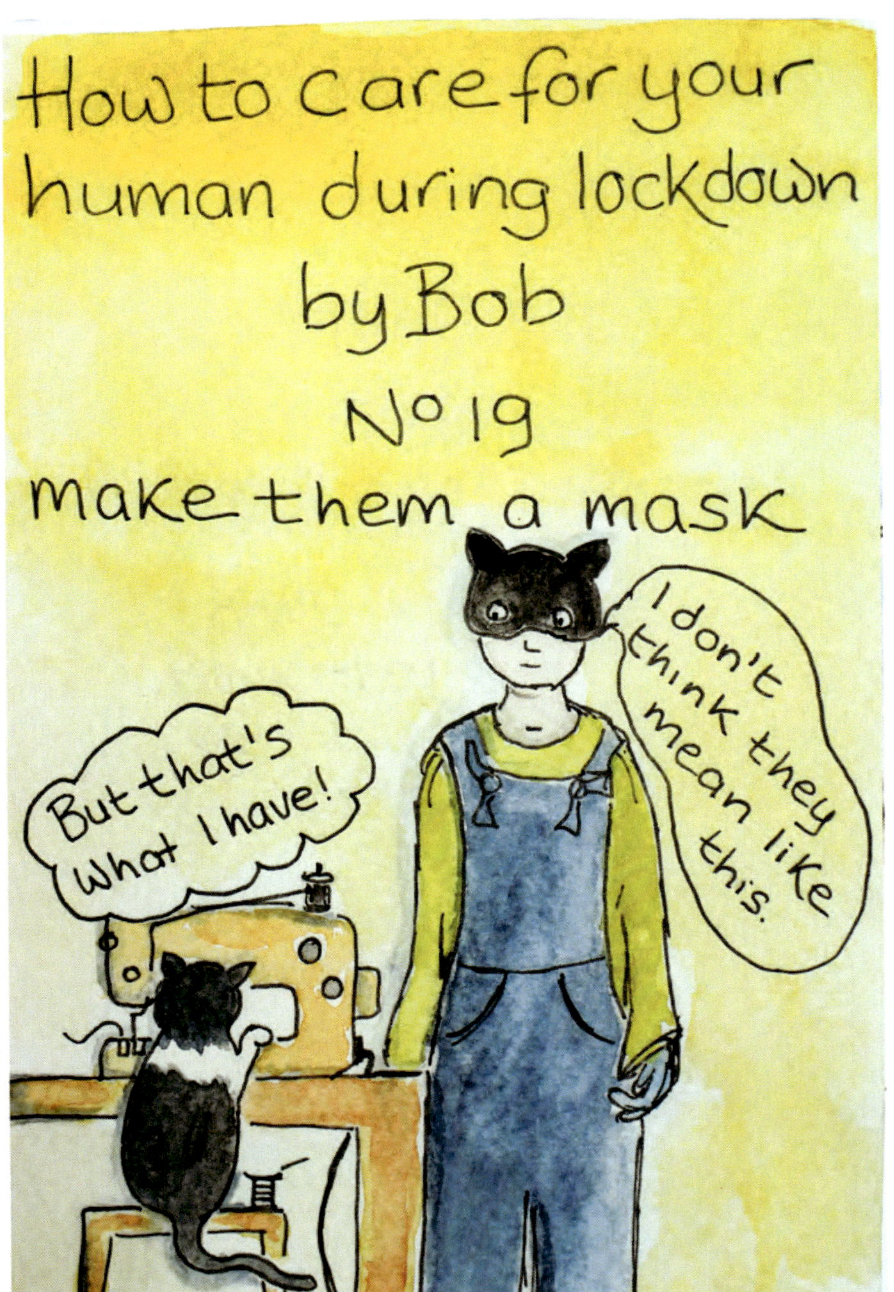
How to care for your human during lockdown
by Bob
No 19
make them a mask
I don't think they mean like this.
But that's what I have!

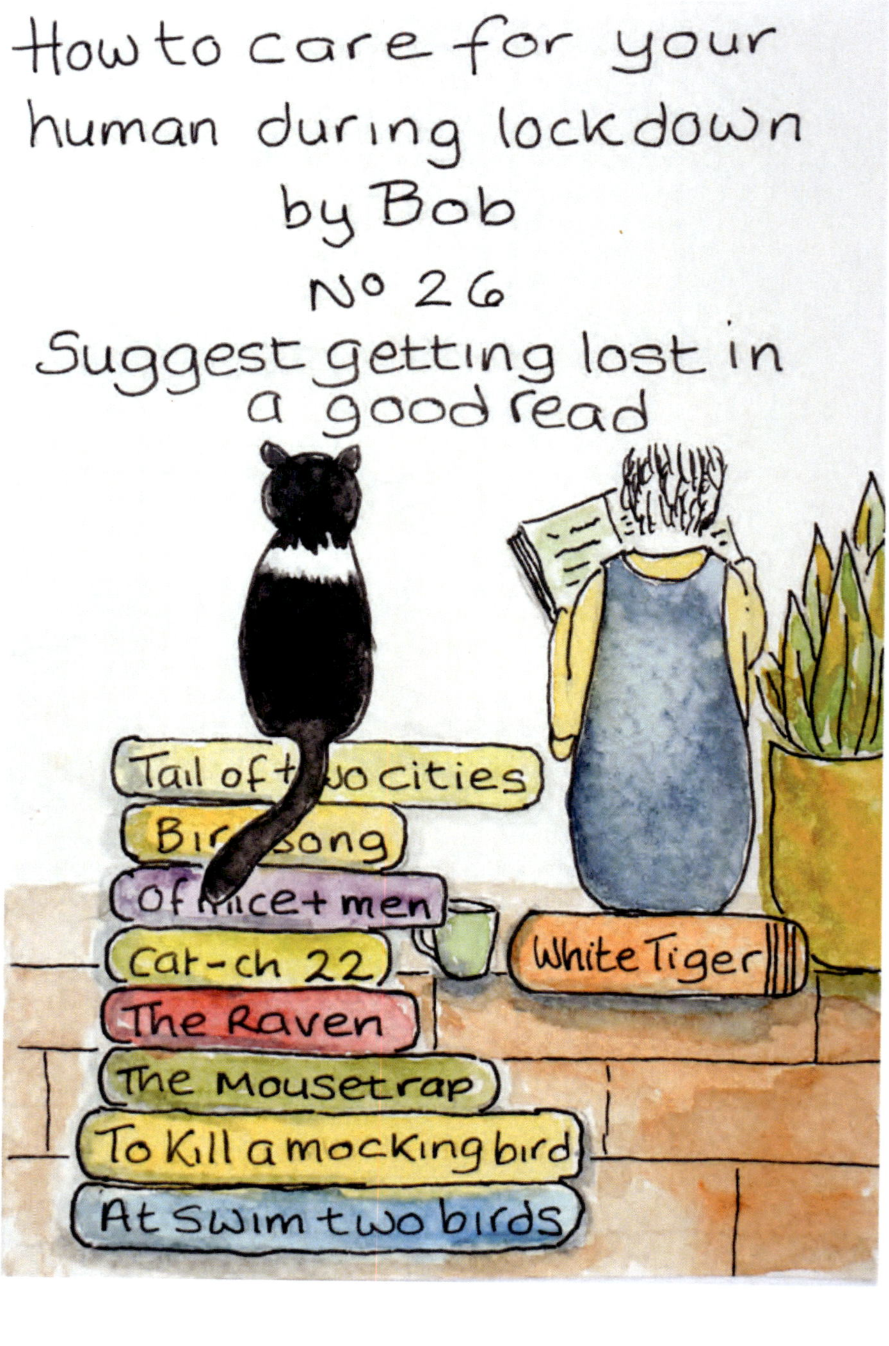

How to care for your human during lockdown by Bob

No 26

Suggest getting lost in a good read

Tail of t wo cities
Bir song
Of ice+men
Cat-ch 22
The Raven
The Mousetrap
To Kill a mocking bird
At Swim two birds
White Tiger

Dear Bob... No 27

What is the difference between social and physical distancing?

(a) Social distancing

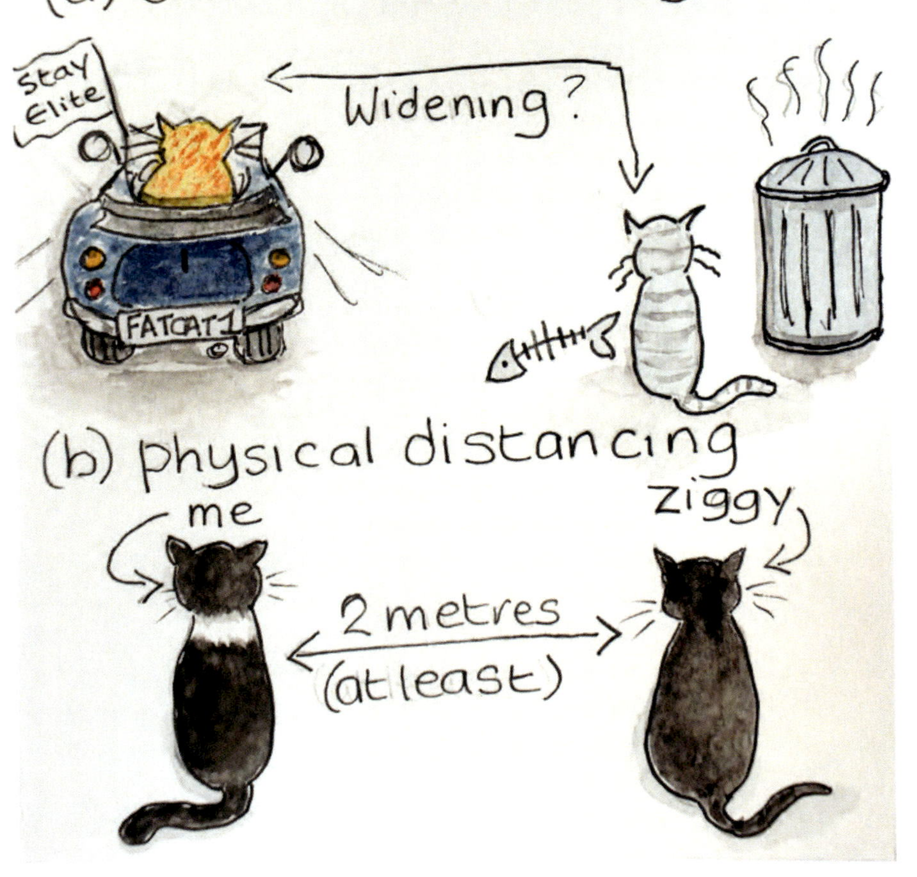

Being Creative

Leisa Taylor

I'm Leisa and I'm nearly 50 years old. I've lived in Worcester for nearly 30 years, hailing originally from a small mining village in West Yorkshire.

I grew up believing that I wasn't very good at art but I really enjoyed creating things. Lockdown for me was an ideal opportunity to slow down and reflect on my life, the world and my place within it. It was a really creative time for me because it was a way of expressing myself and because it was a way of ordering my life in what seemed a very unordered world.

The collages were the result of several zoom workshops run by a friend which I attended religiously every Saturday morning, These quickly became a treasured and valued part of my lockdown routine - again a way of connecting with a community.

Life under Lockdown was meant as a snapshot and celebration of all I had been doing during lockdown - fitness, creativity, gardening, politics, family time - and combined collage with embroidery.

Silver Linings was a 'tear and reveal' collage that represented the virus on the top layer and the 'silver linings' that I felt had been revealed as part of my personal response.

Through doing these my confidence in my artistic abilities grew - and a growing appreciation of 'art for art's sake' which led me to participate in a sketchbook prompt challenge to reproduce an old journal piece that meant a lot to me. *Silver Birch Goddess* was a reproduction of a piece I had done years ago following an experience I had but I'll let the poem speak for this one.

Now lockdown is relaxing and the world has got bigger and busier again. I am already mourning the time I was able to spend creating, but I plan to create space for me to do more in the future.

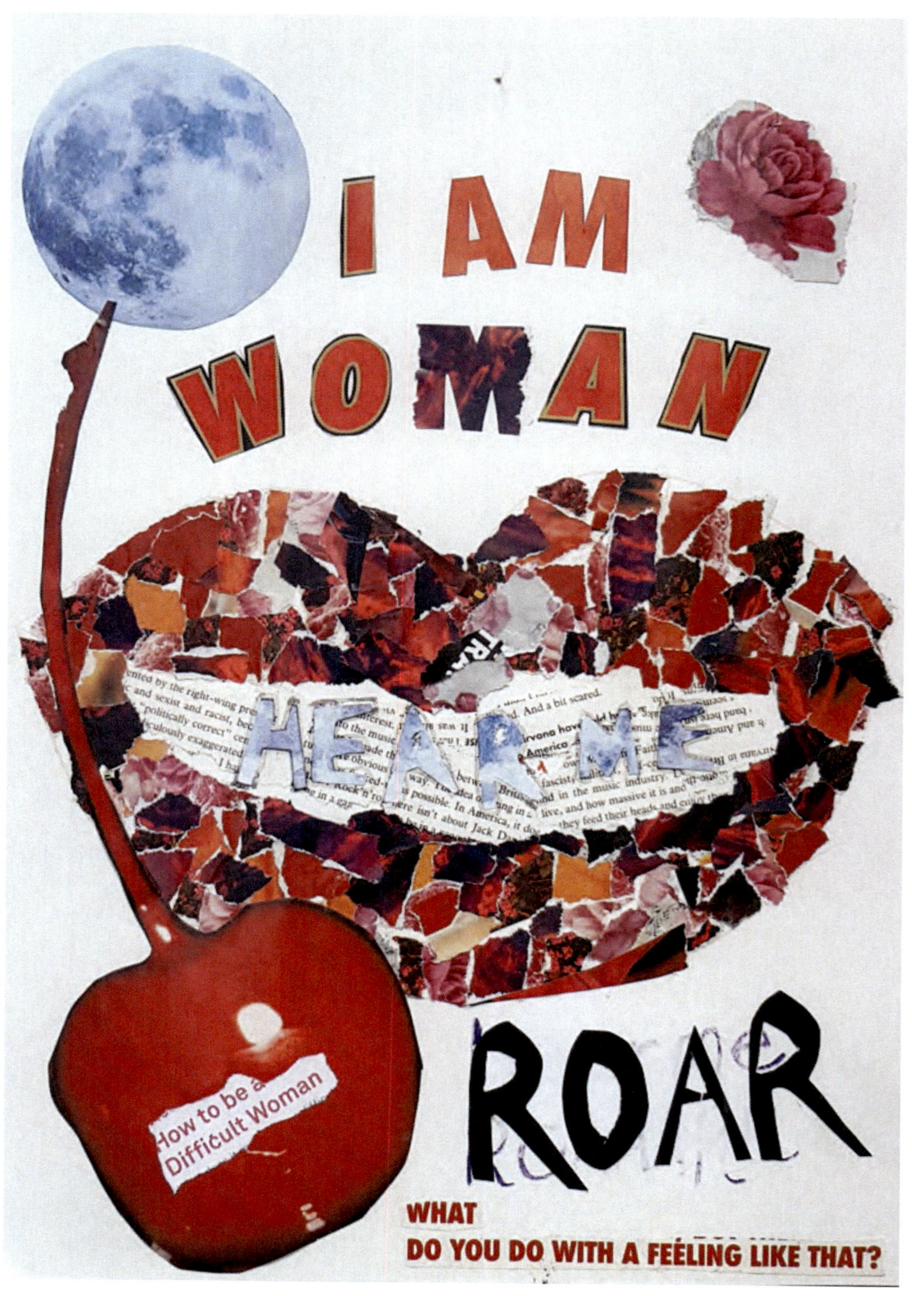
I AM
WOMAN
HEAR ME
ROAR
How to be a
Difficult Woman
WHAT
DO YOU DO WITH A FEELING LIKE THAT?

Roar

Roar (left) was completed at the end of a week where my daughter had experienced her first period and her first curb crawl. It was such a juxtaposition for me to be saying 'Welcome to Womanhood' and all that that entails.

Don't Blow It, Robin was a piece inspired by my political affiliation to the Women's Equality Party and a campaign we were running around care workers and the Immigration Bill.

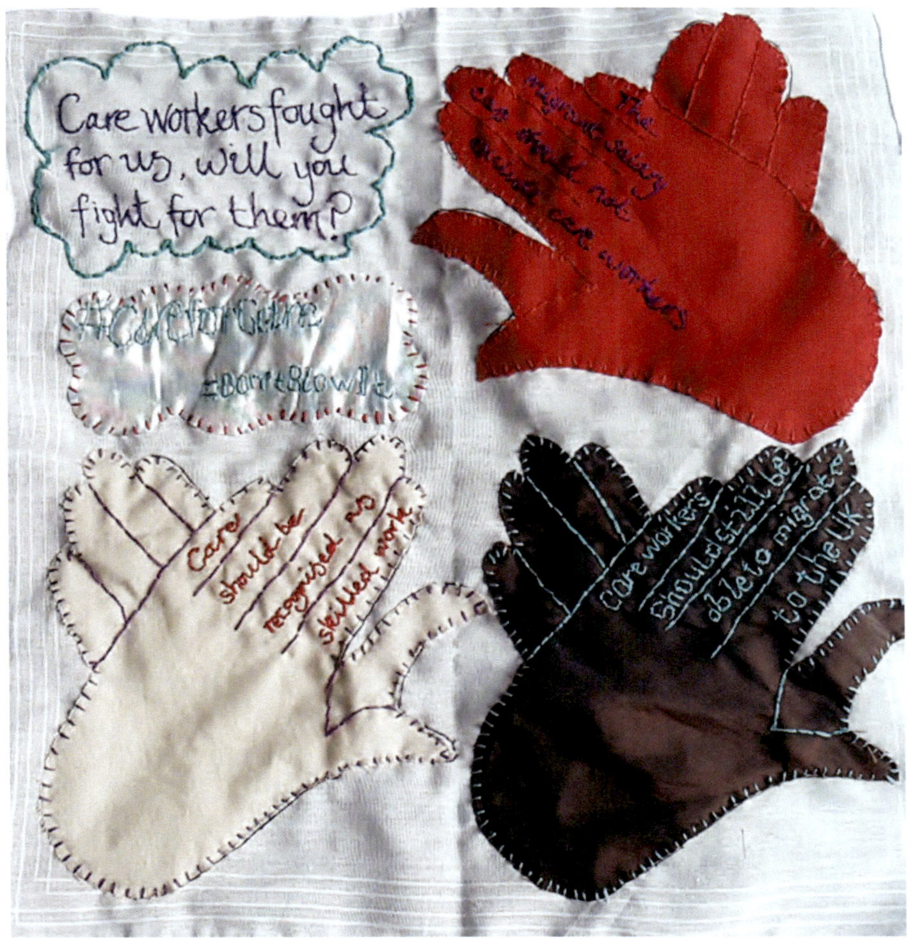

Don't Blow It, Robin

Dear Robin Walker was part of a Young Women's Trust art challenge for their campaign 'No Young Woman Left Behind'. I sent this and *Don't Blow It, Robin* with a letter to Robin Walker, MP.

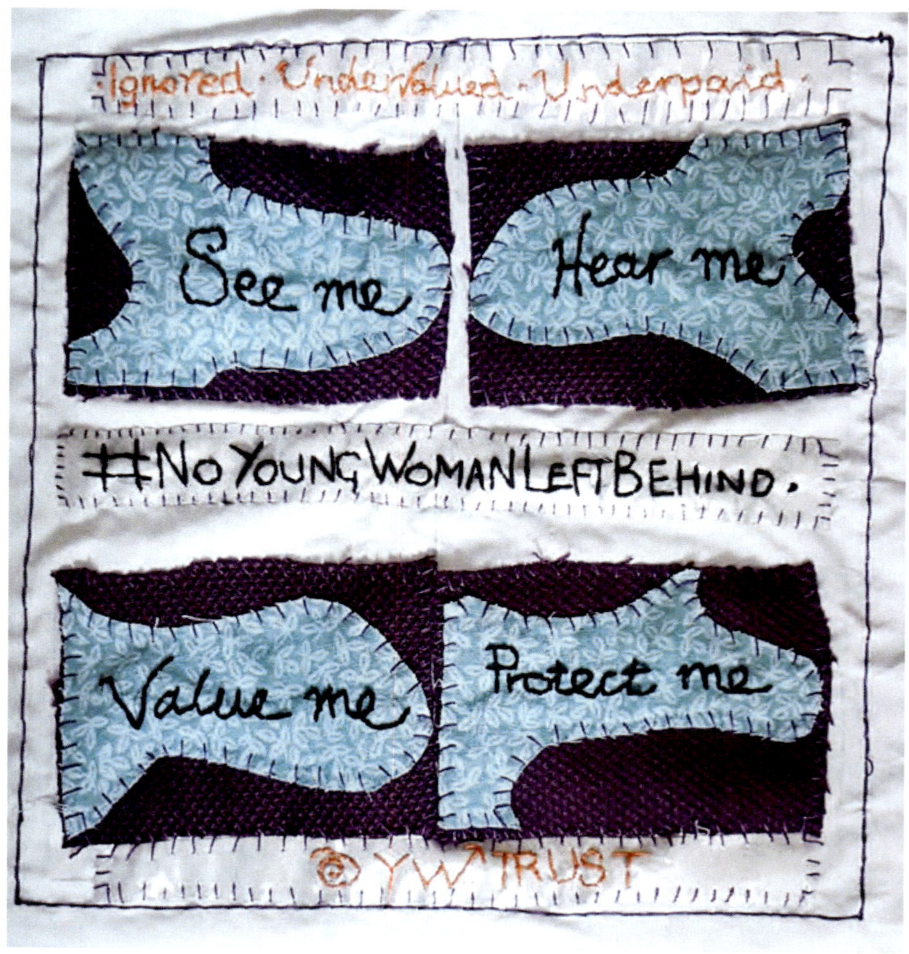

Dear Robin Walker

Girl's Best Friend (right) is a card I made for my daughter featuring her and our puppy (a goddess-send for our lockdown) it was an attempt at combining collage as applique.

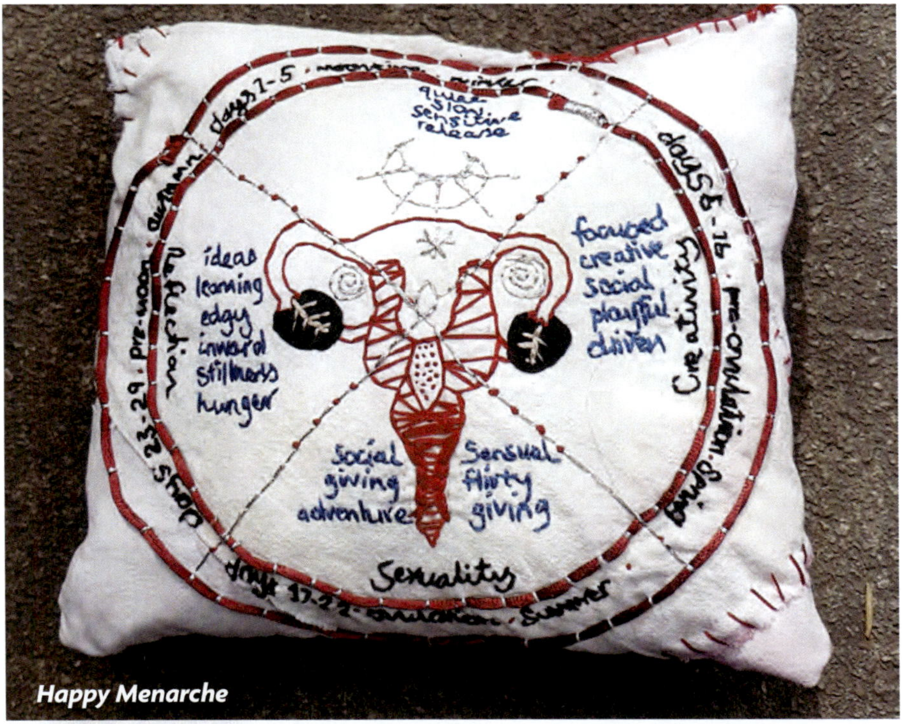

Happy Menarche

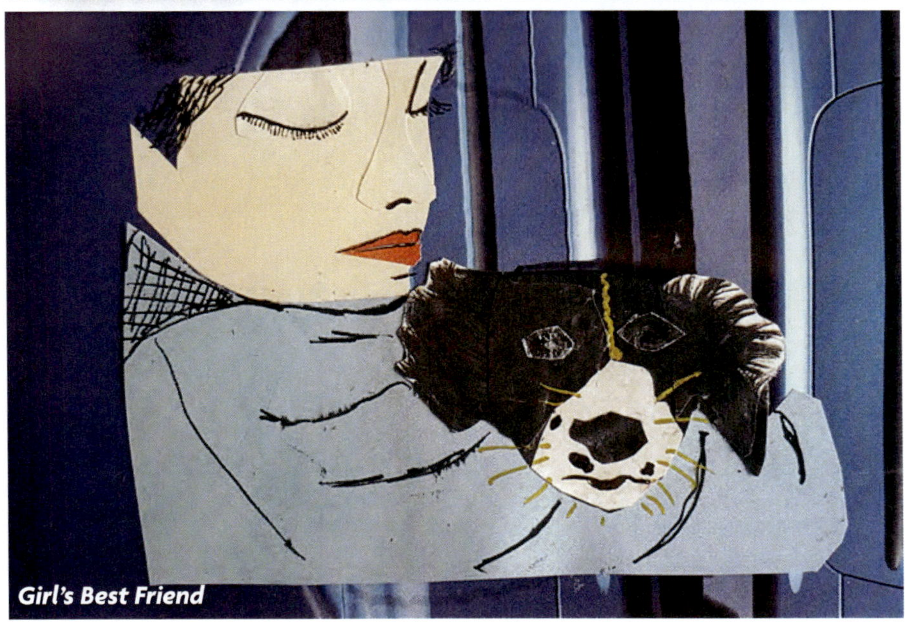

Girl's Best Friend

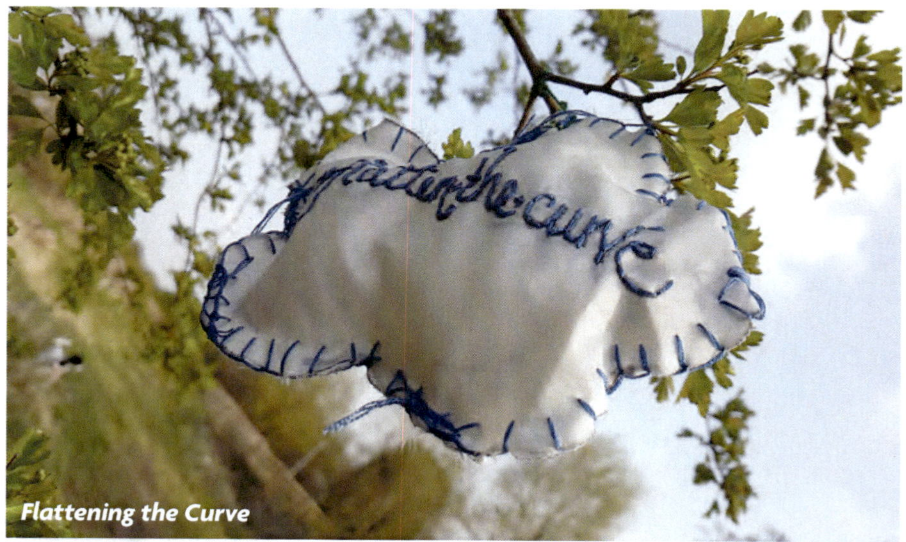

Flattening the Curve

Flatten The Curve and *Wash Your Hands But Not of Each Other* were my response to the narratives circulating at the beginning of lockdown and also to the strong feelings of concern I was feeling for the vulnerable and lonely. The embroidered mobiles were my way of reaching out to my community in a positive way - I discovered 'craftivism' a few years ago and it is such a gentle but powerful way of raising awareness and expressing opinions.

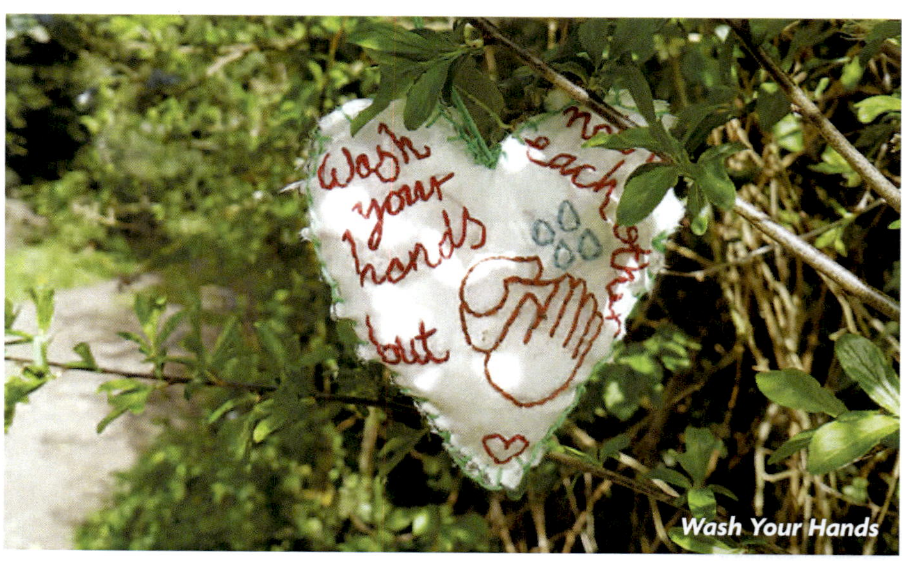

Wash Your Hands

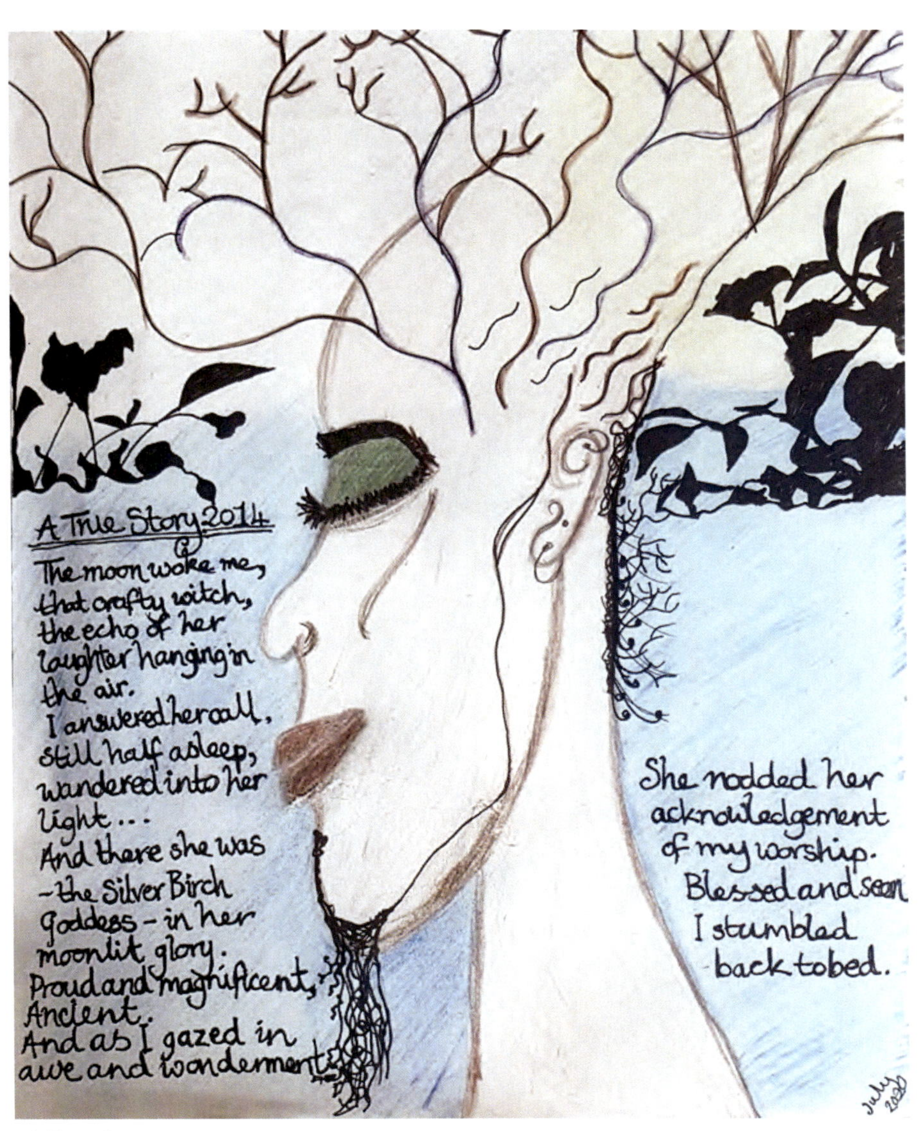
A True Story 2014
The moon woke me,
that crafty witch,
the echo of her
laughter hanging in
the air.
I answered her call,
still half asleep,
wandered into her
light...
And there she was
- the Silver Birch
Goddess - in her
moonlit glory.
Proud and magnificent,
Ancient.
And as I gazed in
awe and wonderment
She nodded her
acknowledgement
of my worship.
Blessed and seen
I stumbled
back to bed.
July
2020

A True Story

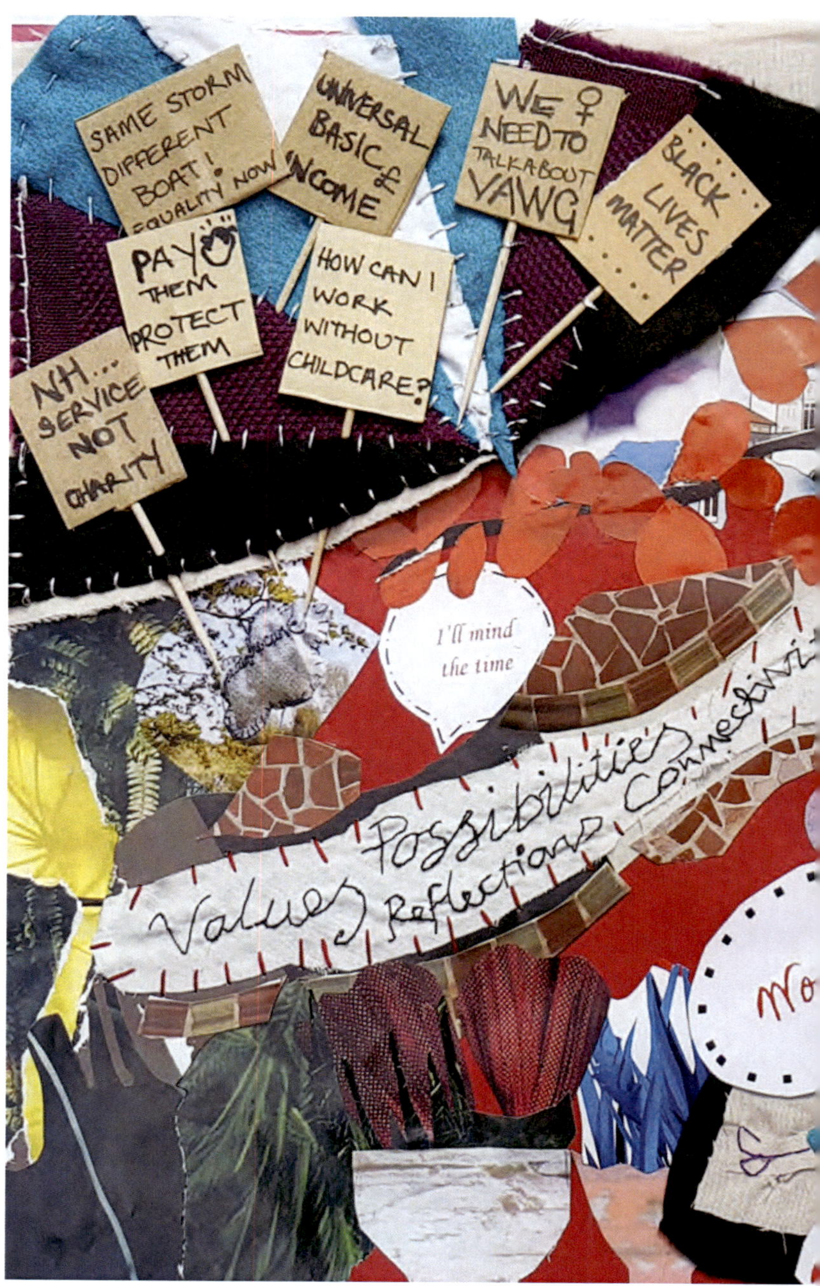

Life In Lockdown

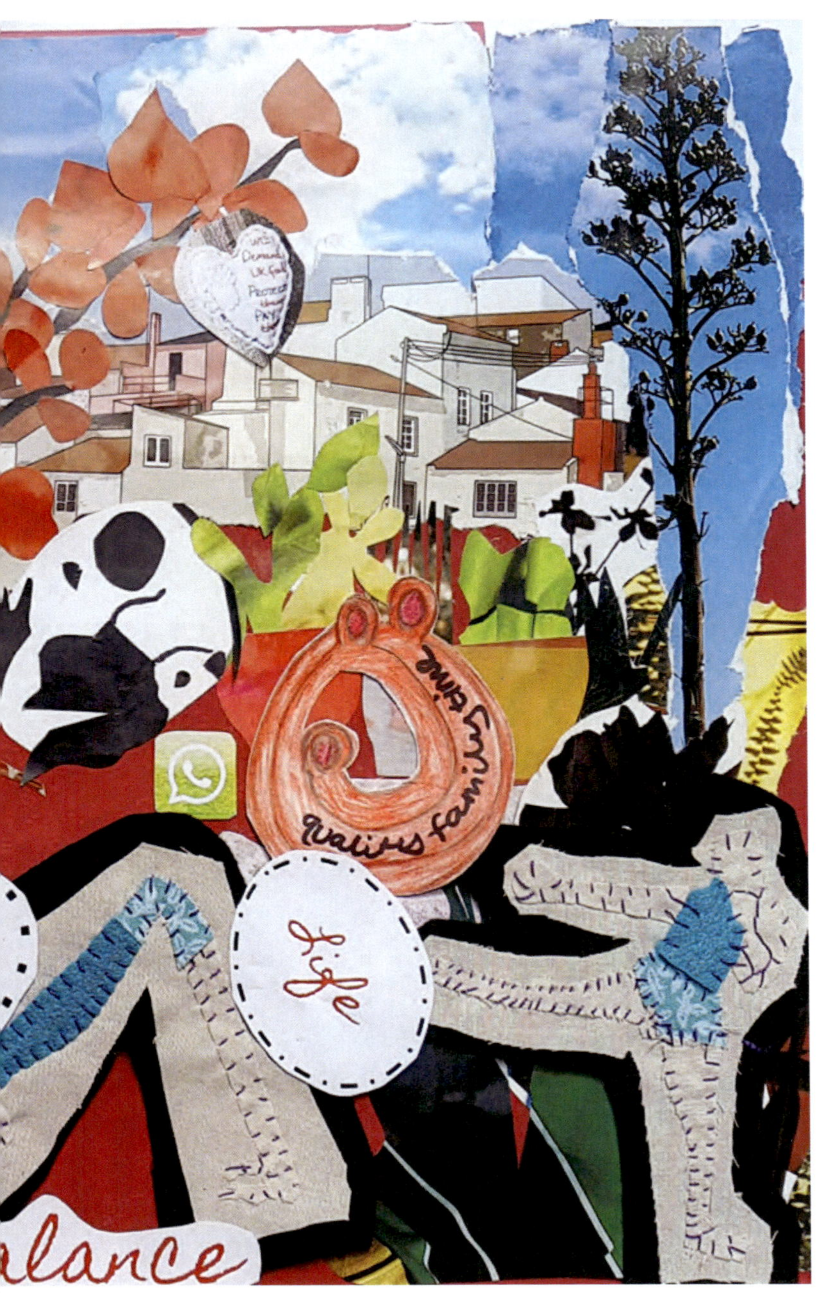
quality family time
life
alance

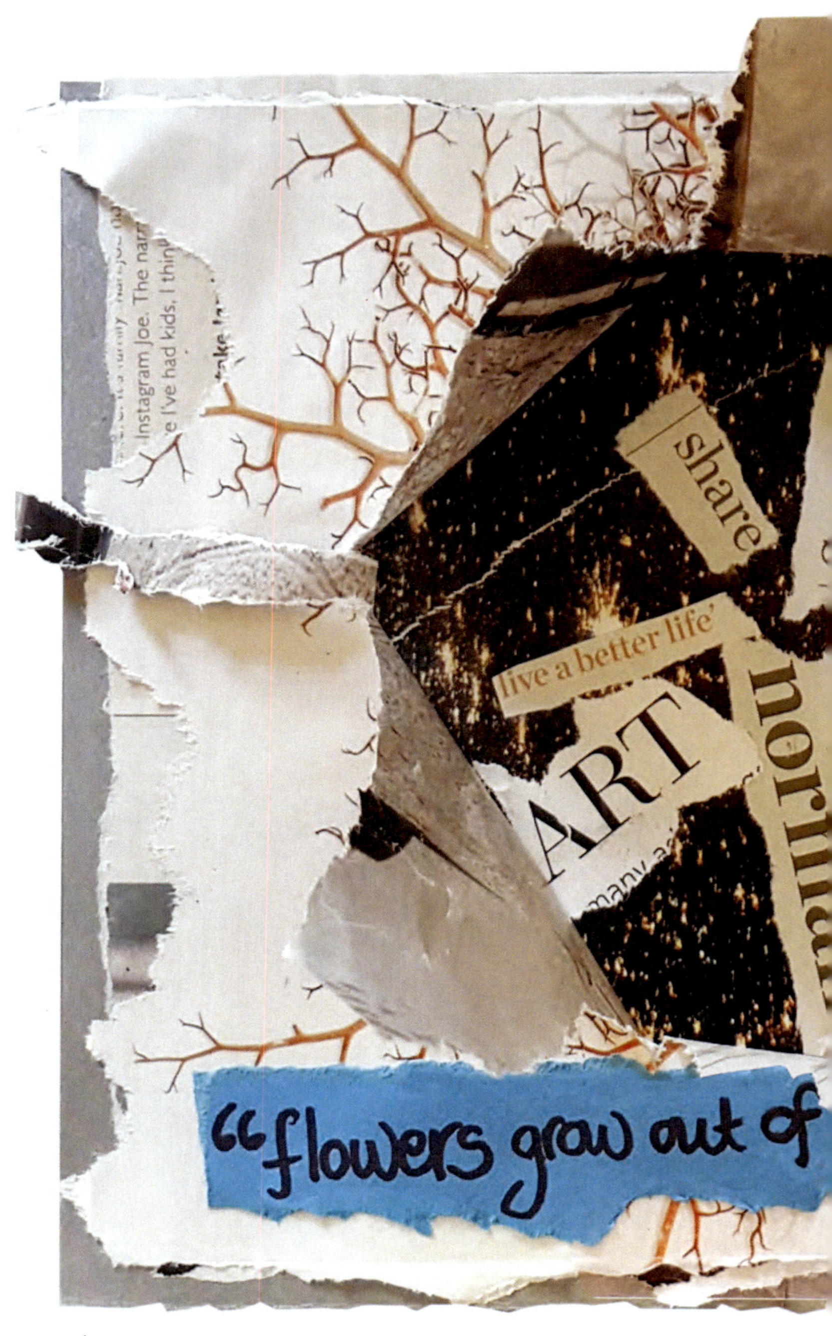

Silver Linings

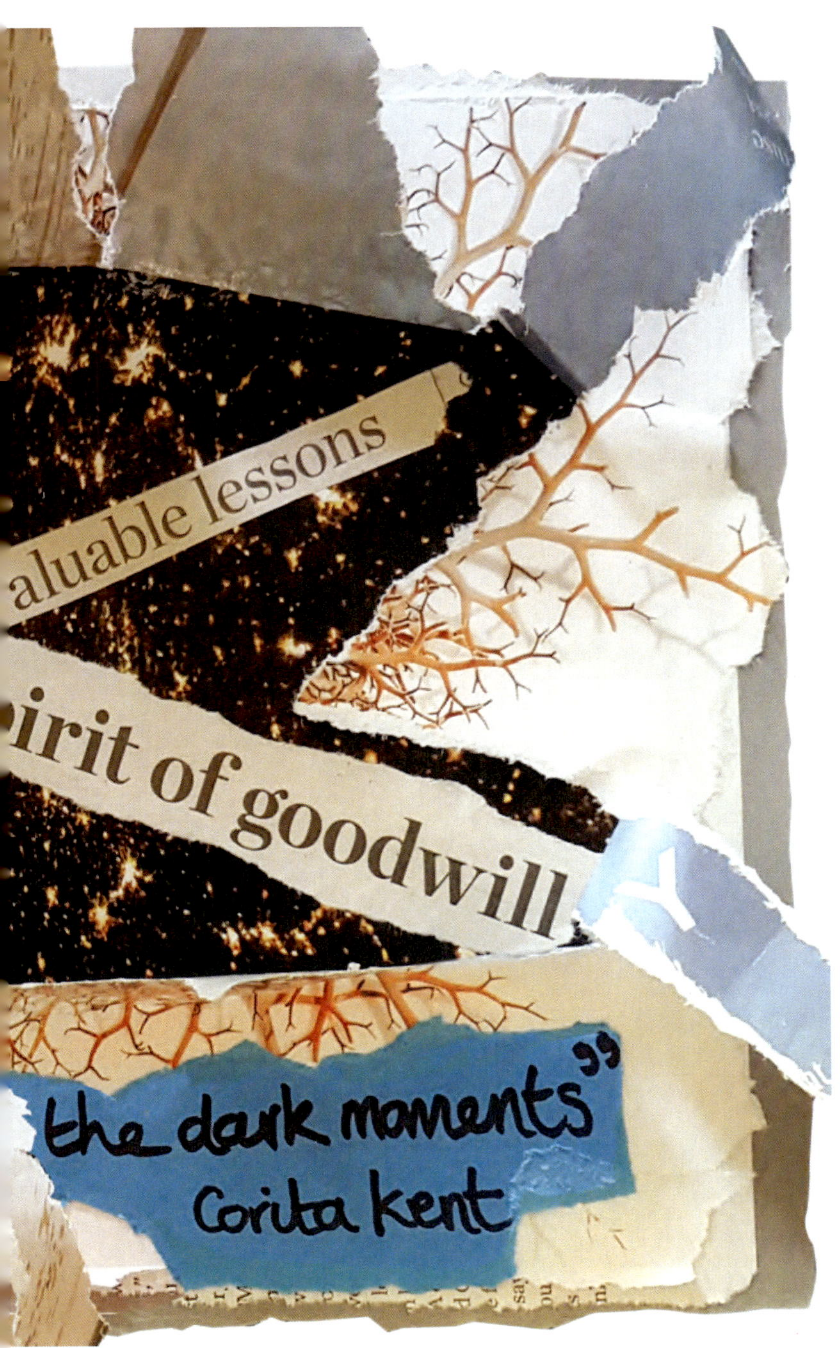
aluable lessons
irit of goodwill
the dark moments"
Corita Kent

10 Squared

Lucy Dennison

Lockdown wasn't a shock to my way of life. Having been diagnosed with severe heart failure a year before, my life had become restricted. COVID-19 felt like the world was now moving at my steady pace. The quiet and calm helped my creative urges to bloom again.

I'm a retired early years teacher and very interested in children's creativity being fostered through playing with materials and having no fear about getting it "wrong". Lockdown became a time for me to follow my own philosophy and get on with making art and feeling like an artist who creates for her own pleasure. I still love tearing and gluing and working in mixed media.

During lockdown my cats became my muses. I wanted to capture the kitten's extraordinarily feisty personality. I love lino printing and made a very basic design of fearsome Freda. I've been able to adapt it playing with colour and printing media.

I used chalks, paints, tissue paper, just like art in the nursery class. I added natural materials to the mix in the collage"Spruce".

Lockdown enabled me to have the time to play with my art and to have fun with it with no fear!

Every child is an artist.
The problem is how to remain an artist once we grow up.
Picasso

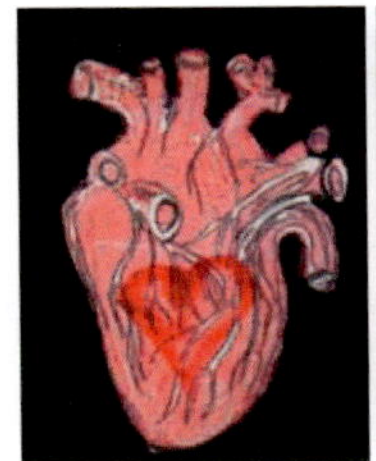
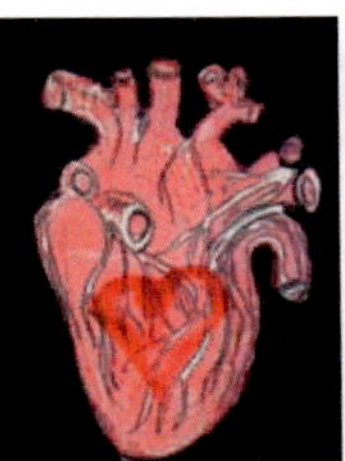
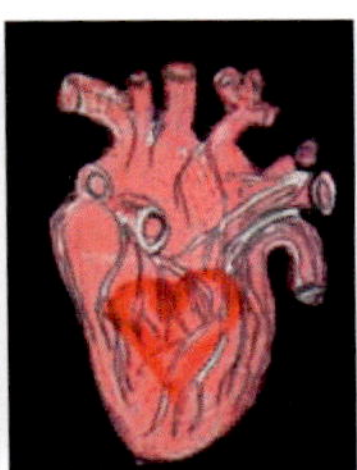
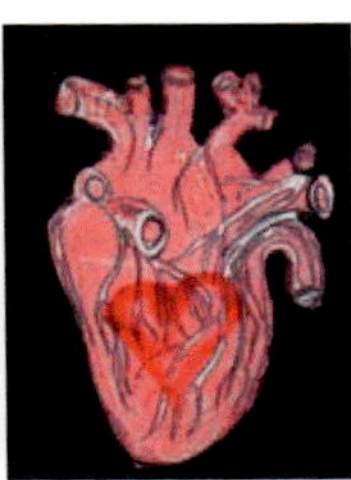
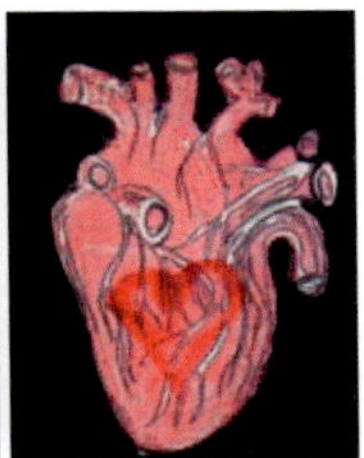

Growth

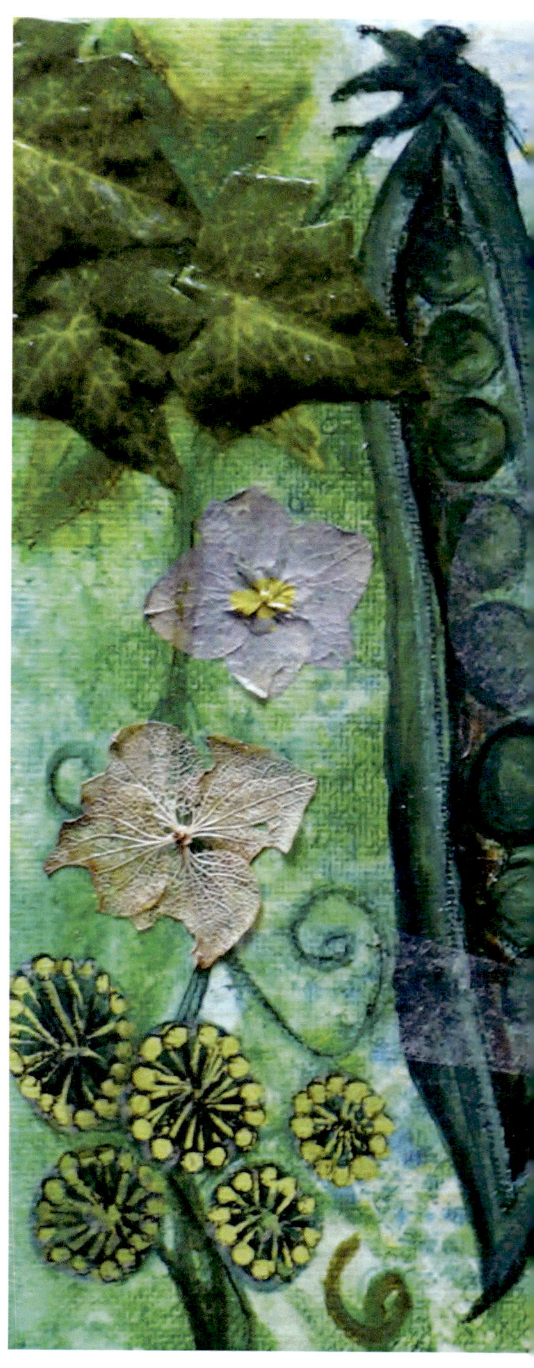

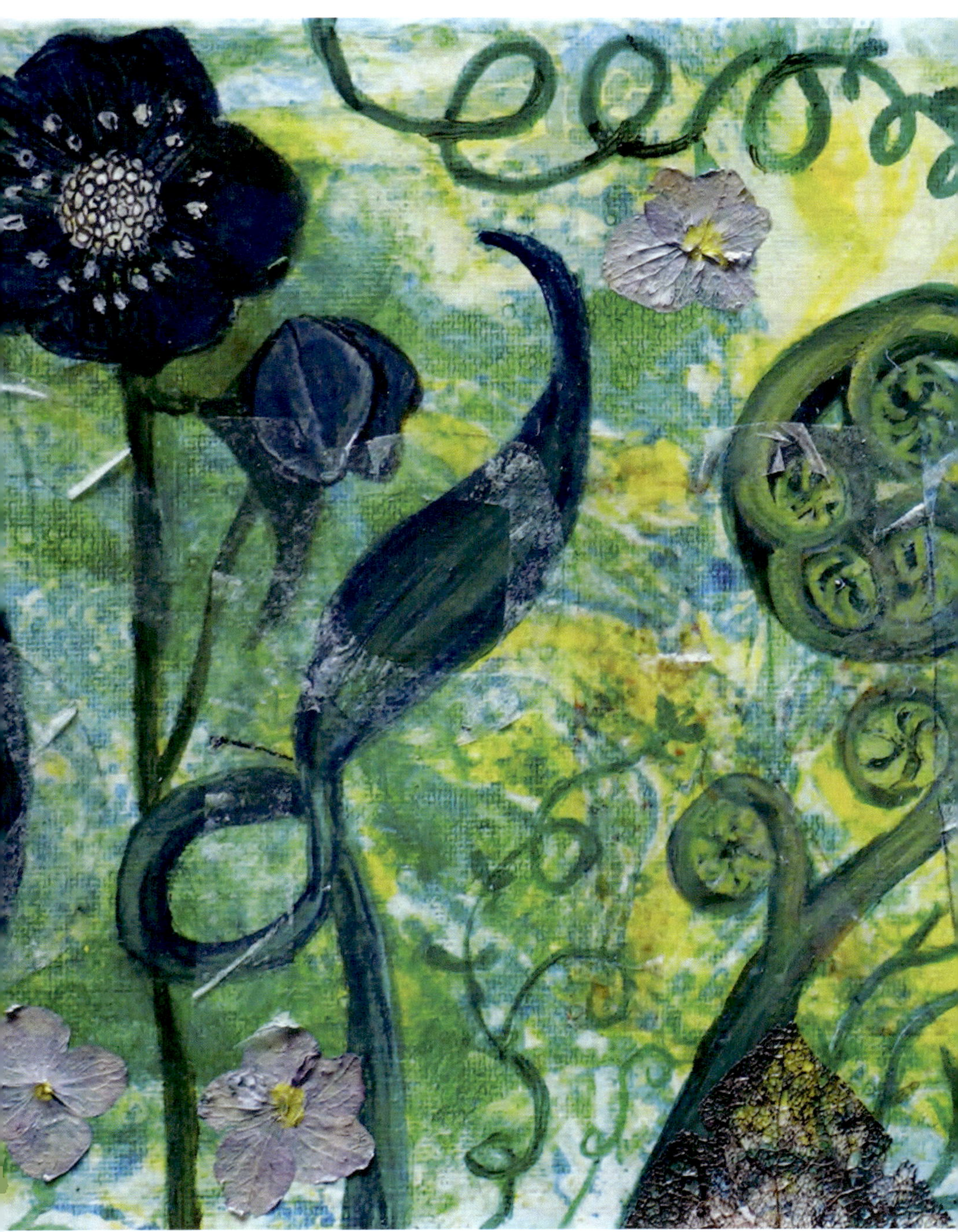

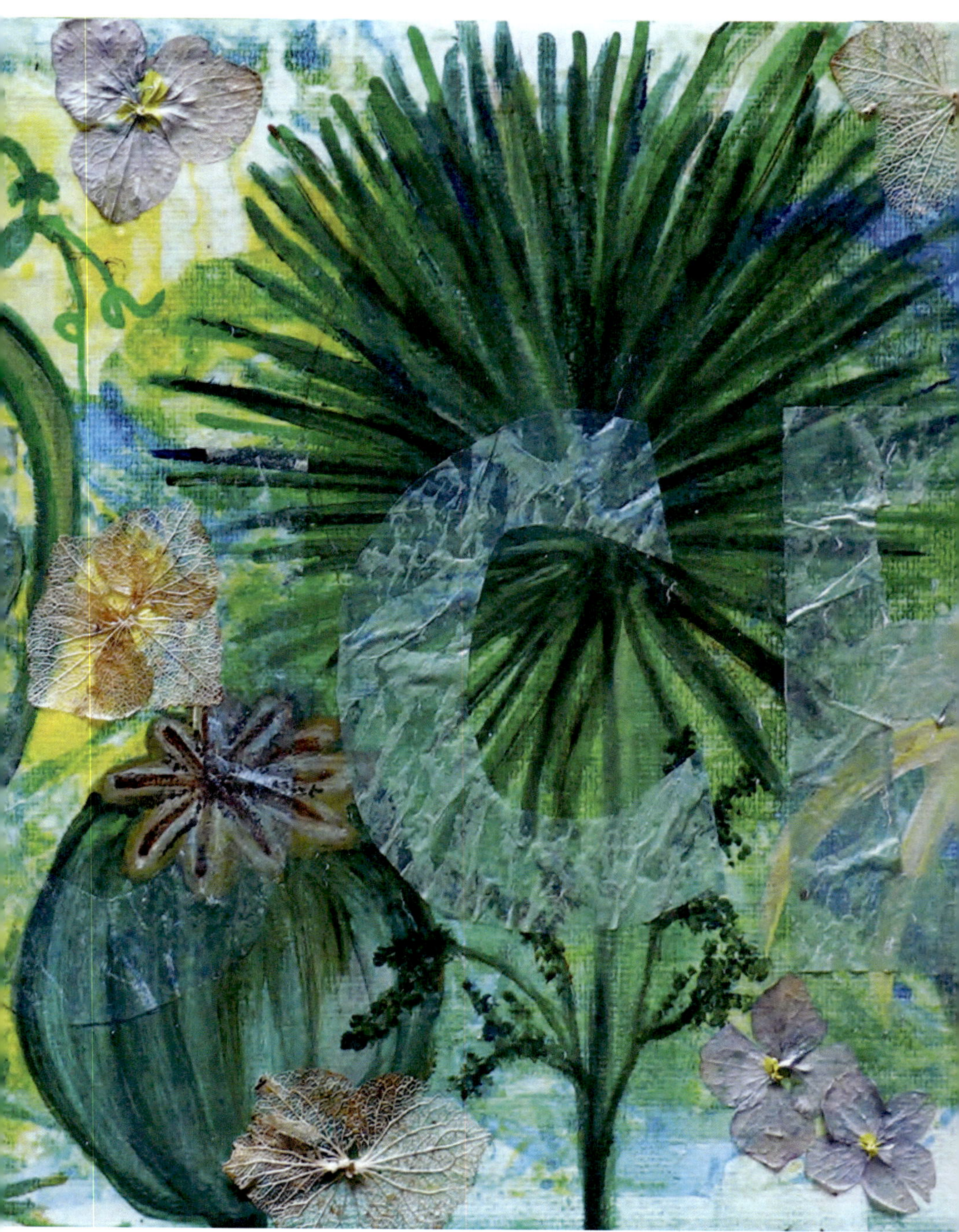

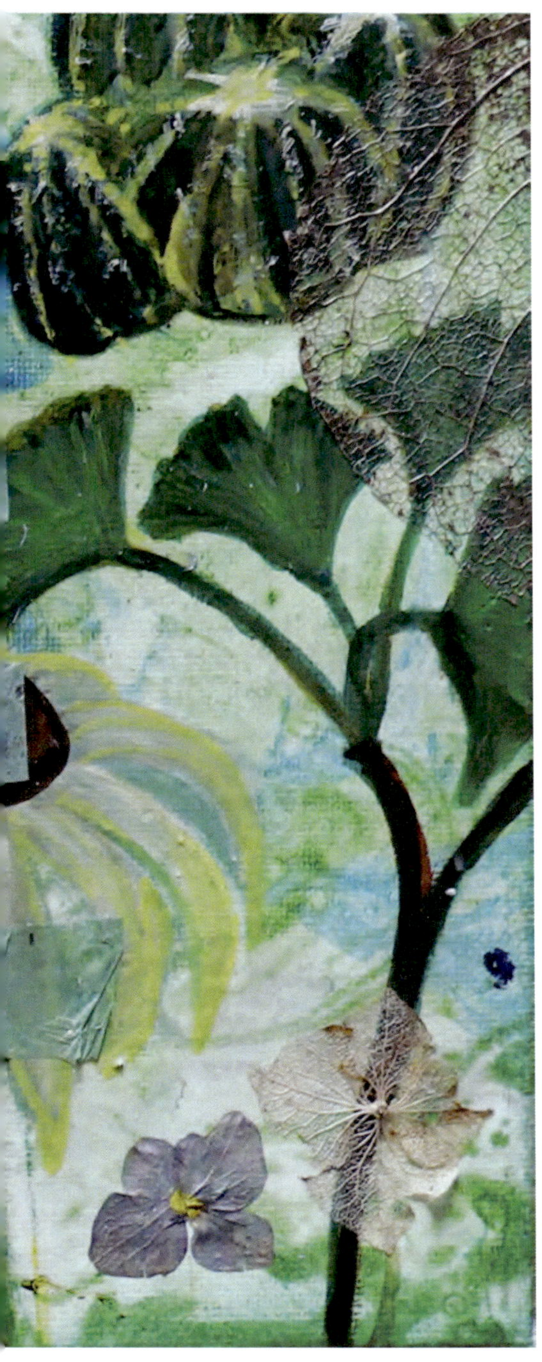

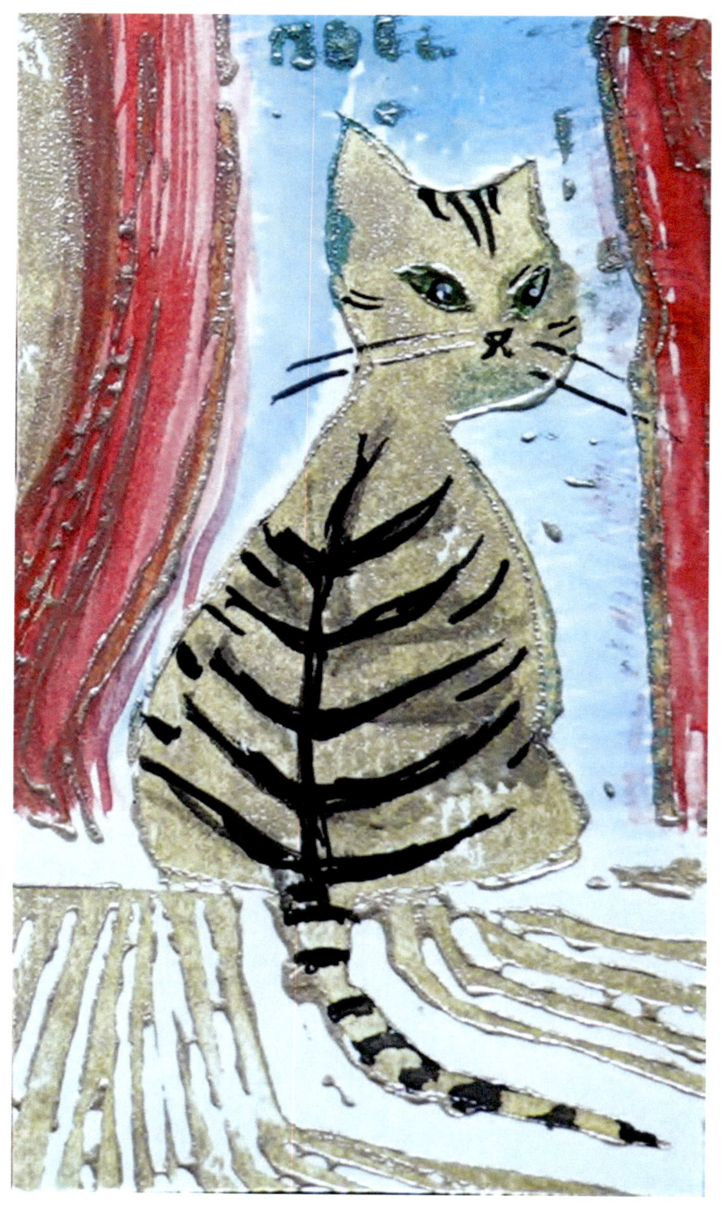

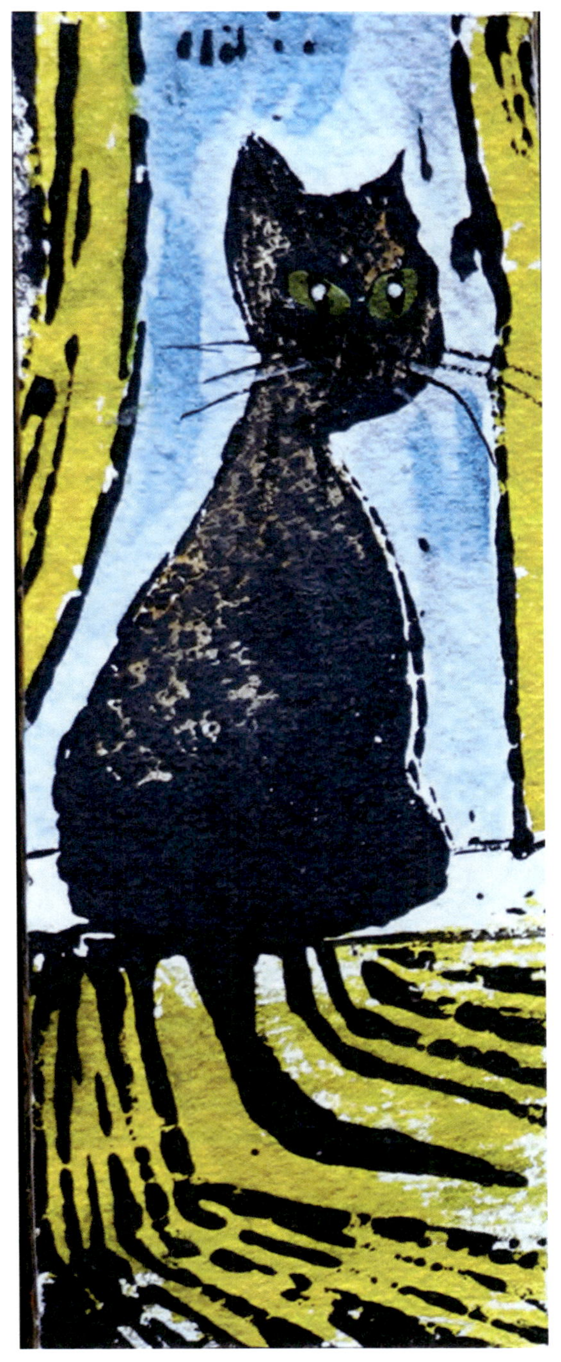

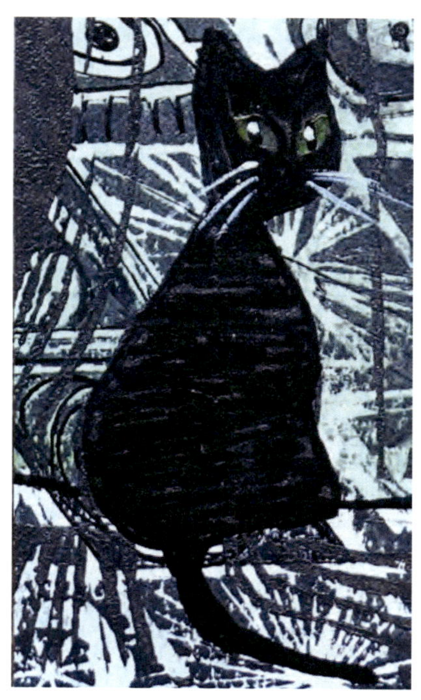

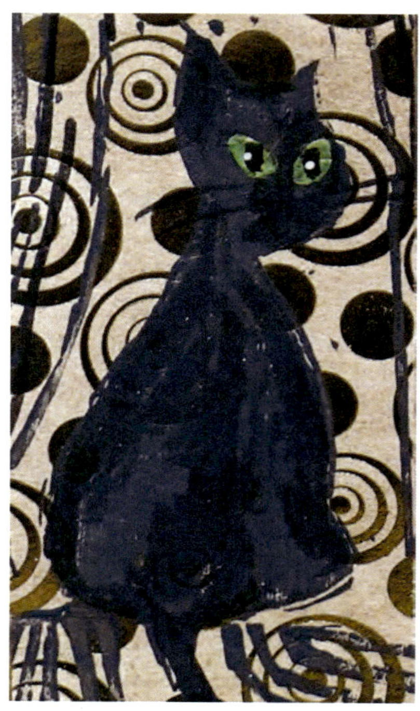

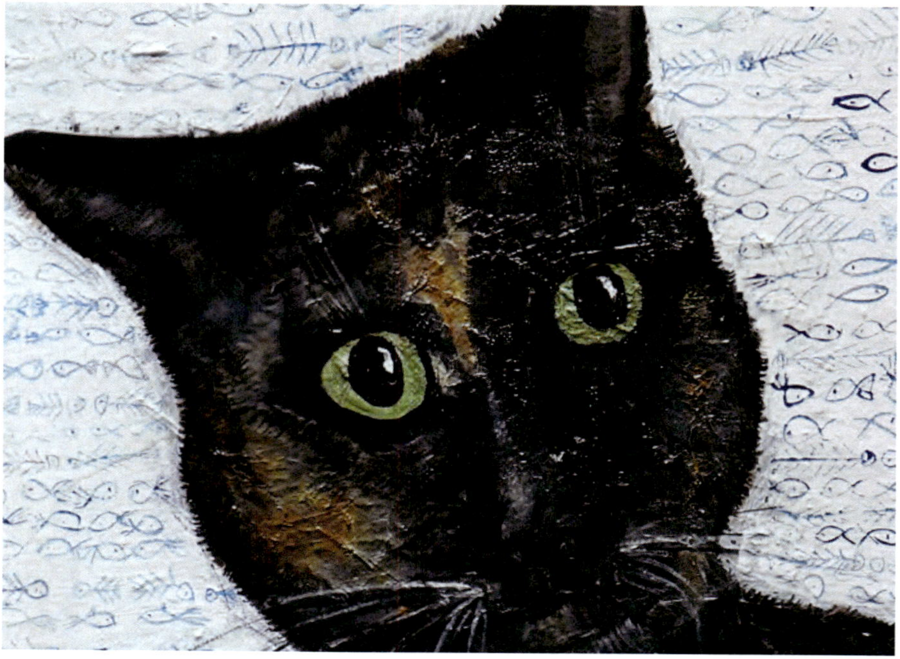

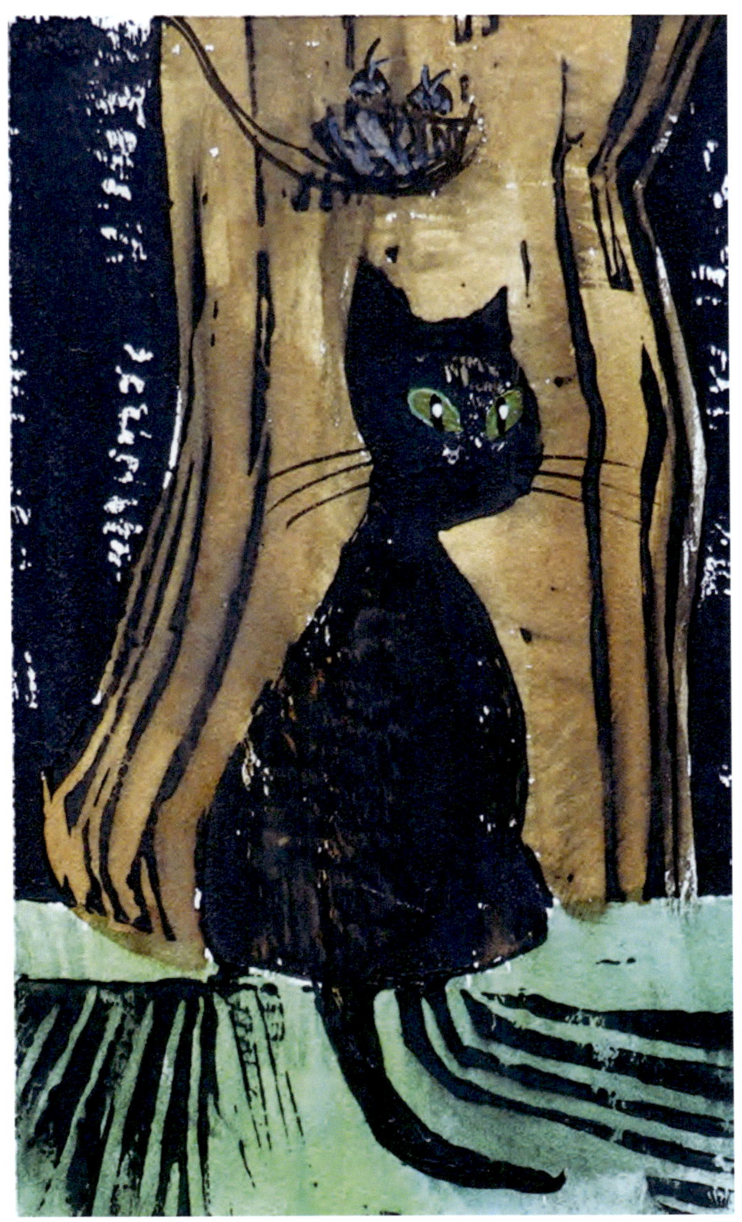

Freda continued to be my muse during lockdown.

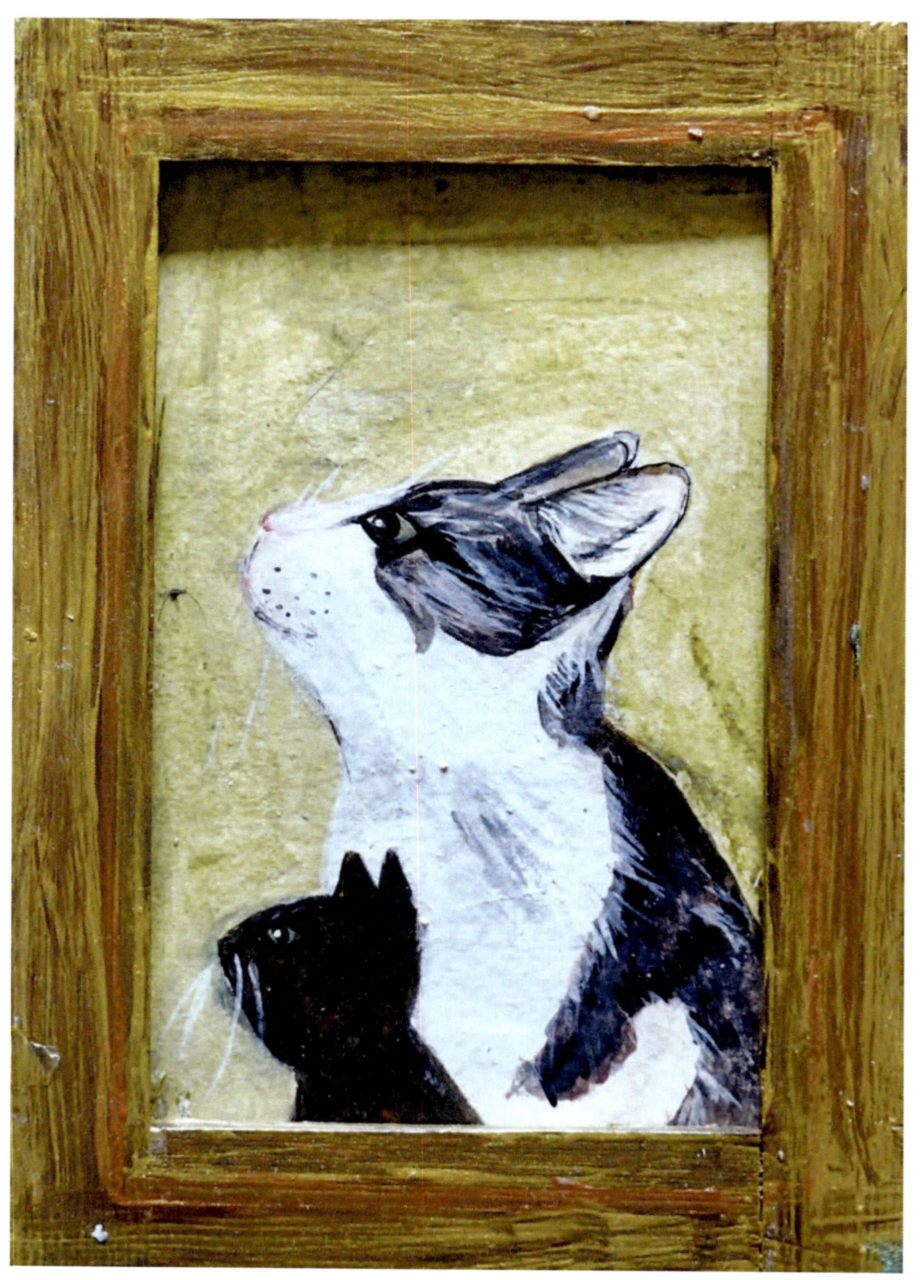

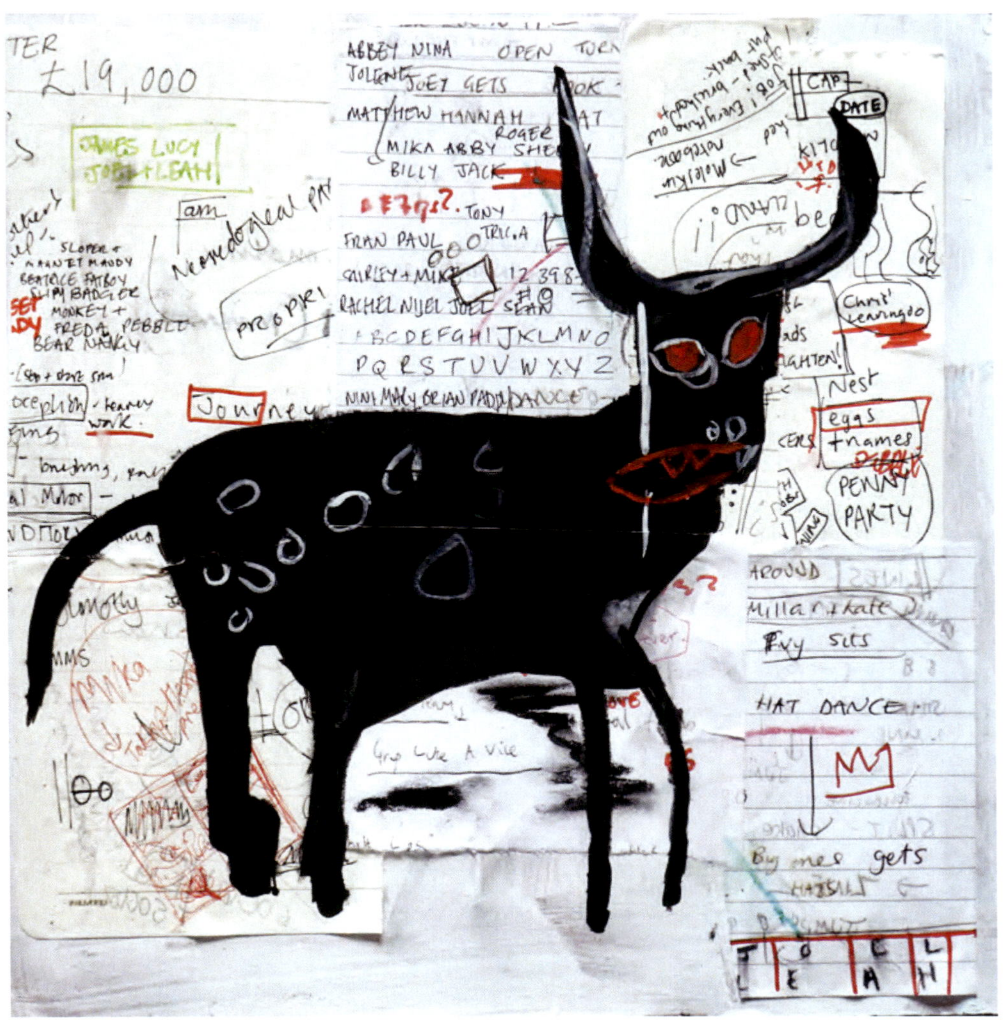

Bull

When teaching I always encouraged looking at and copying other artists. I had great joy and no qualms about copying and adapting Basquiat's "Bull" a request from my husband.

Exercise of the Day

Maggie Keeble

To cope in times of stress we need an inner strength and resilience. This has never been more important than during the Covid pandemic, especially for those of us who work in the NHS. There was a need to maintain mental and physical wellbeing to continue working despite facing some of the most stressful situations I've ever experienced.

At the start of lockdown, as a GP working with older people and those living in care homes, I knew I needed to keep active physically and mentally during this difficult time. I started running early every morning before getting down to work.

What came as a surprise was the creativity that emerged when I began to take photographs on my phone while I was out and posting sets of them on Facebook. It became a real joy collating and sharing something on a regular basis which, from the feedback I received, people obviously enjoyed and appreciated. To start with, I had a totally random approach and was very dependent on light levels in the early morning. Later on, themes started to emerge and I went looking for shots, meaning I was running longer distances. There is no doubt that I felt a pressure to maintain the output which ensured that I went out every day without fail

I managed to continue until the lockdown easing was announced and came through the worst of times, physically fitter than ever and mentally intact. So sixty four "Exercise of the Day Shots" were the result. It's been an added bonus to be able to share a small selection with a wider audience in this 10 x 10 publication.

So 64 "Exercise of the Day Shots"...

How to choose only 10?

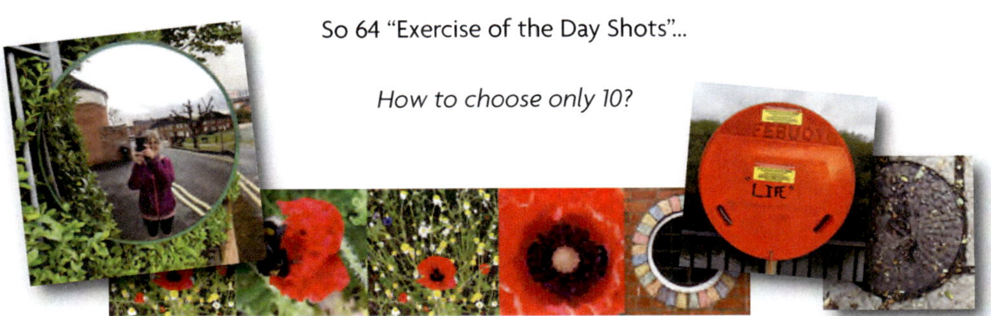

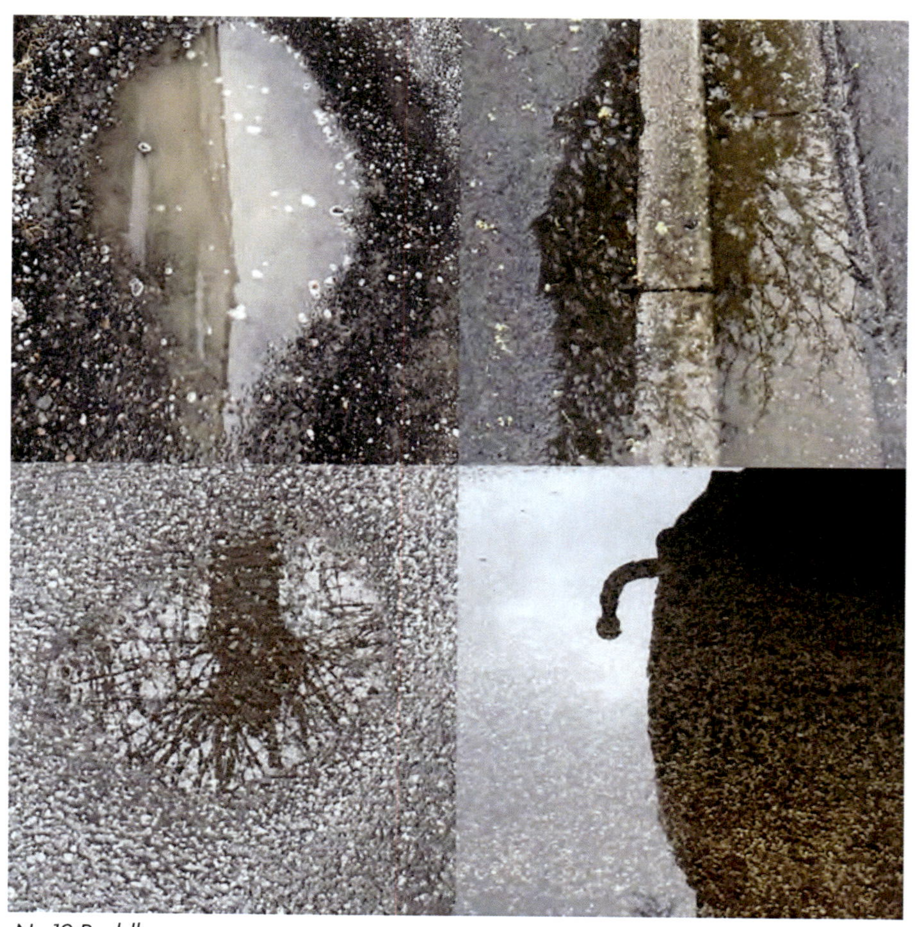

No.19 Puddles

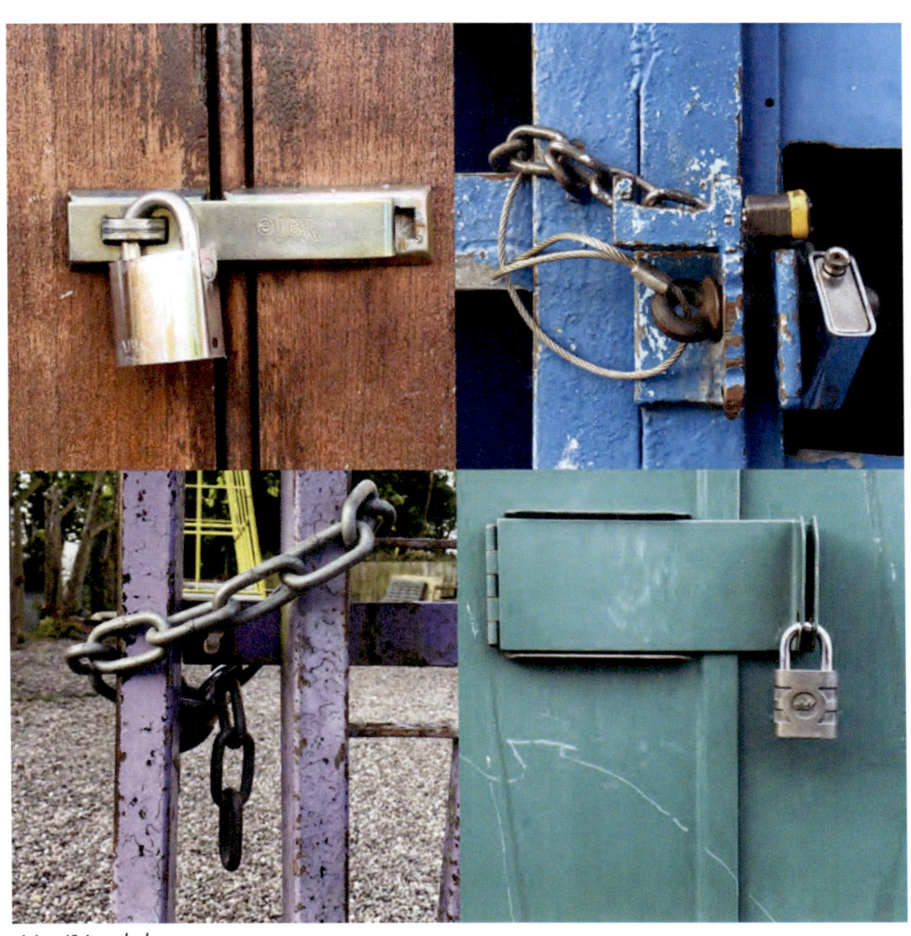

No.41 Lockdown

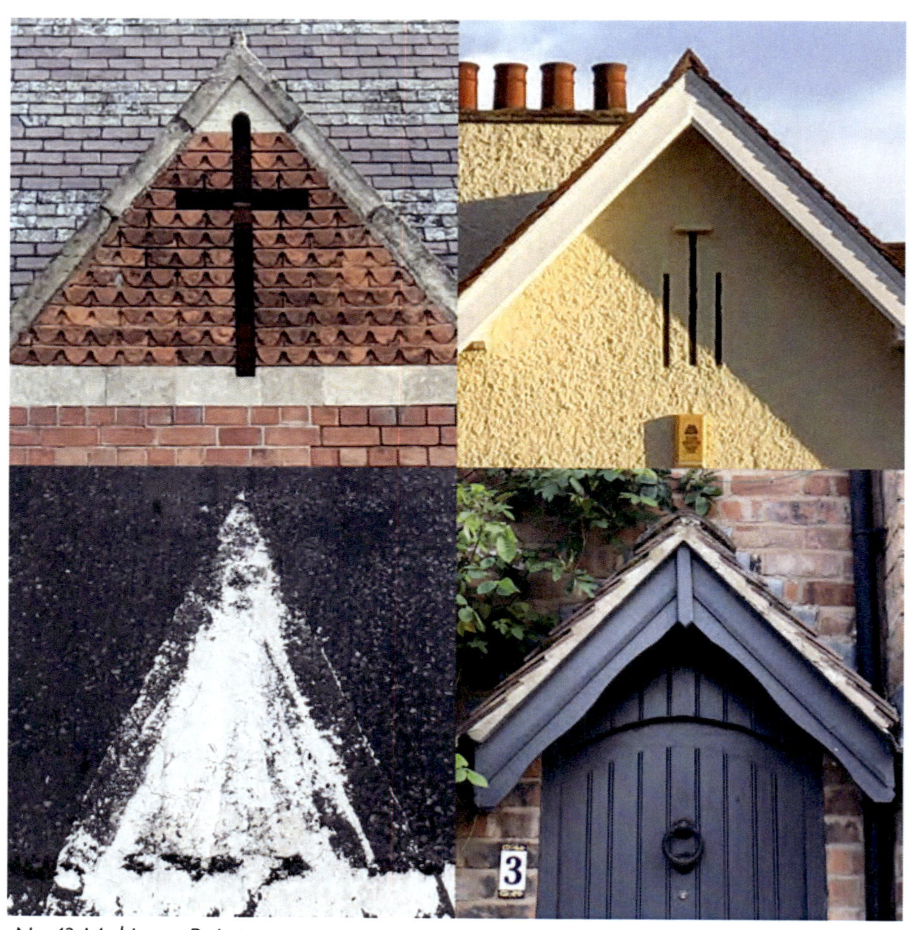

No.43 Making a Point

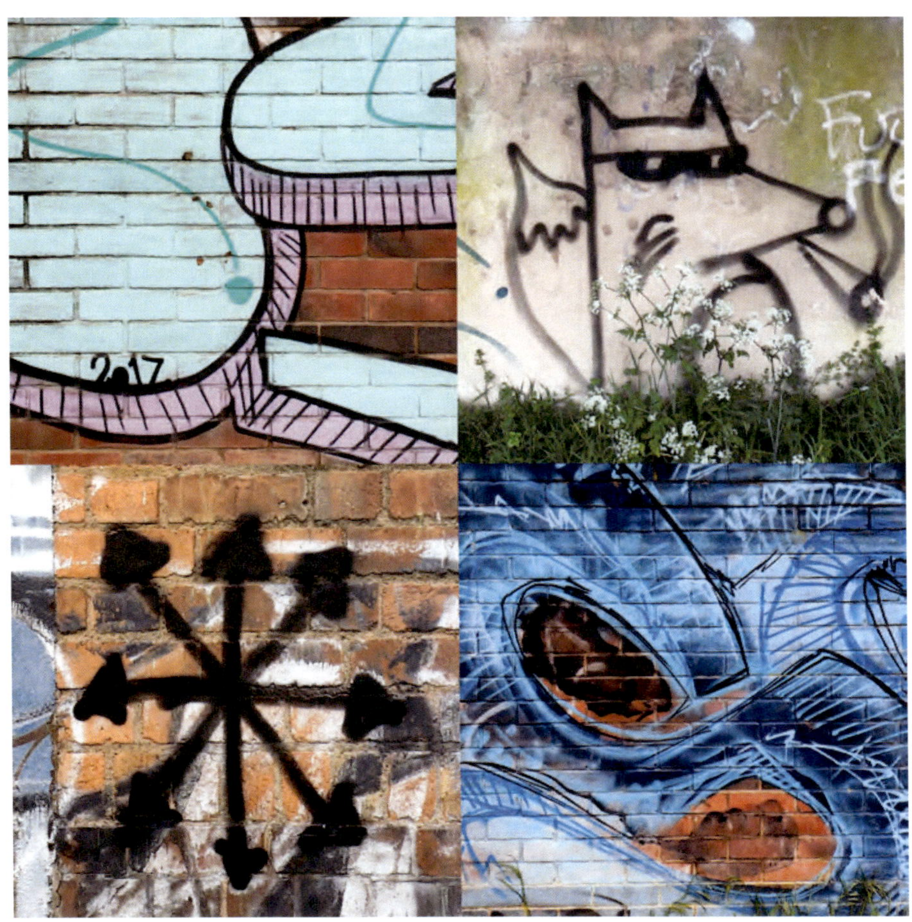

No.46 Graffiti

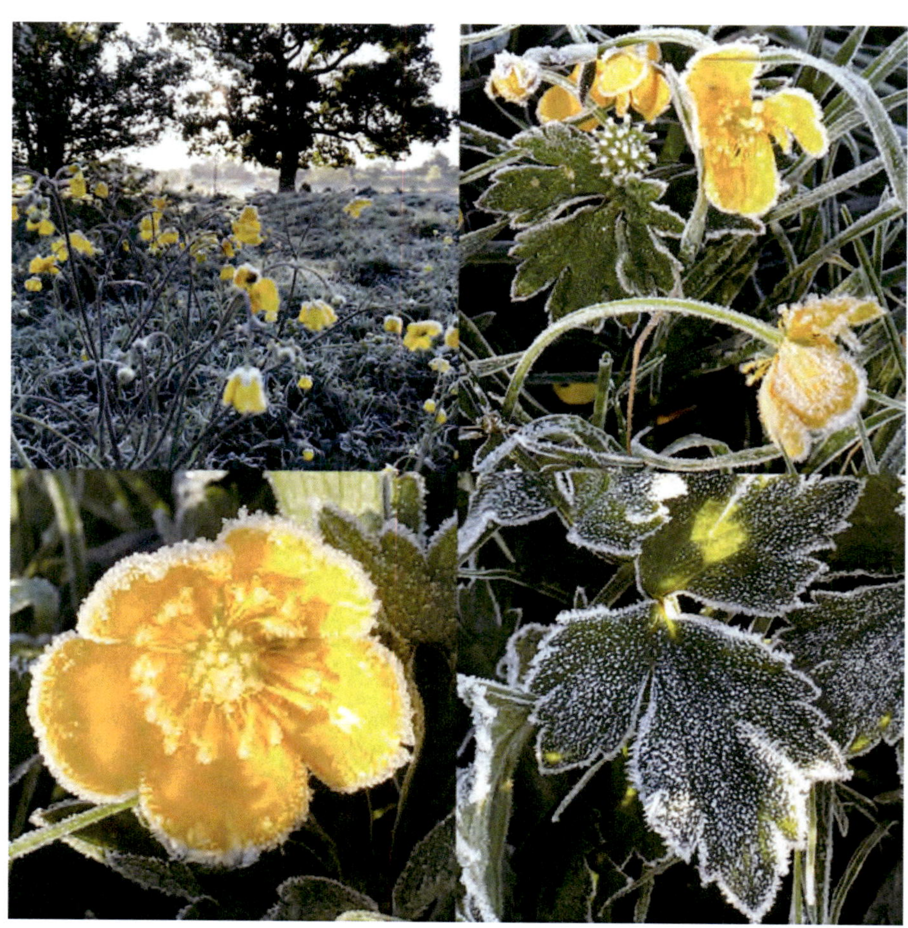

No.48 Frosty Morning on the Lido

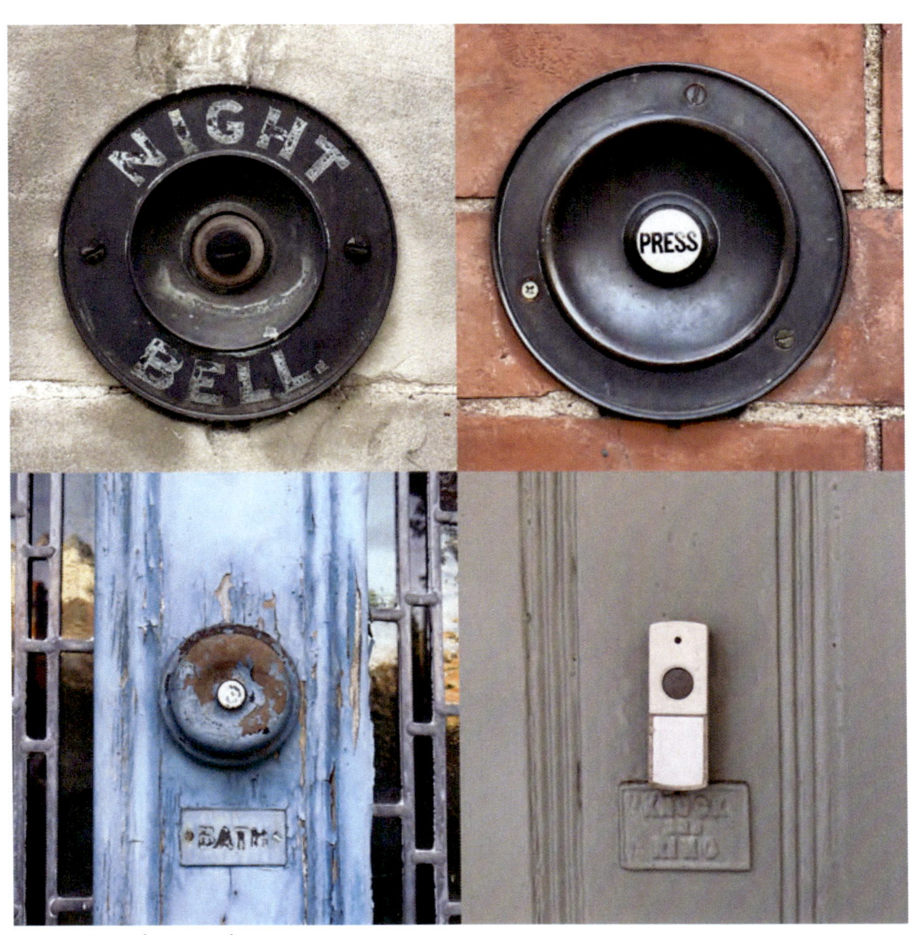

No.54 Hard Pressed

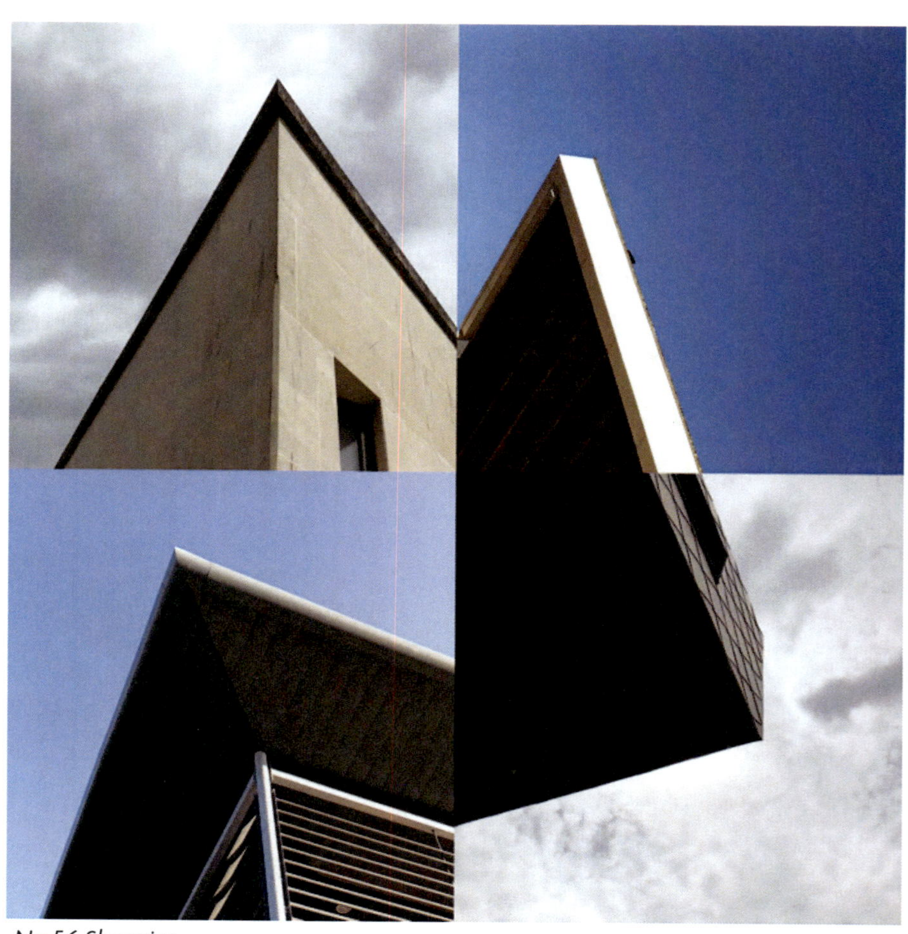

No.56 Sharpies

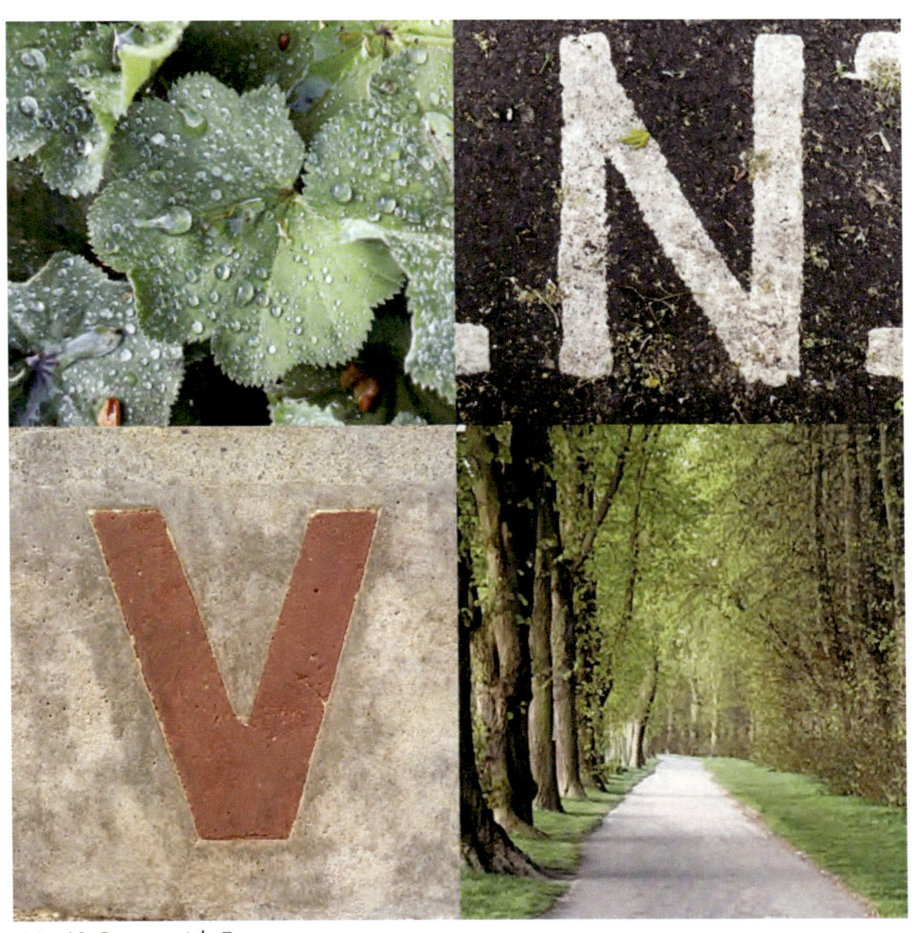

No.60 Green with Envy

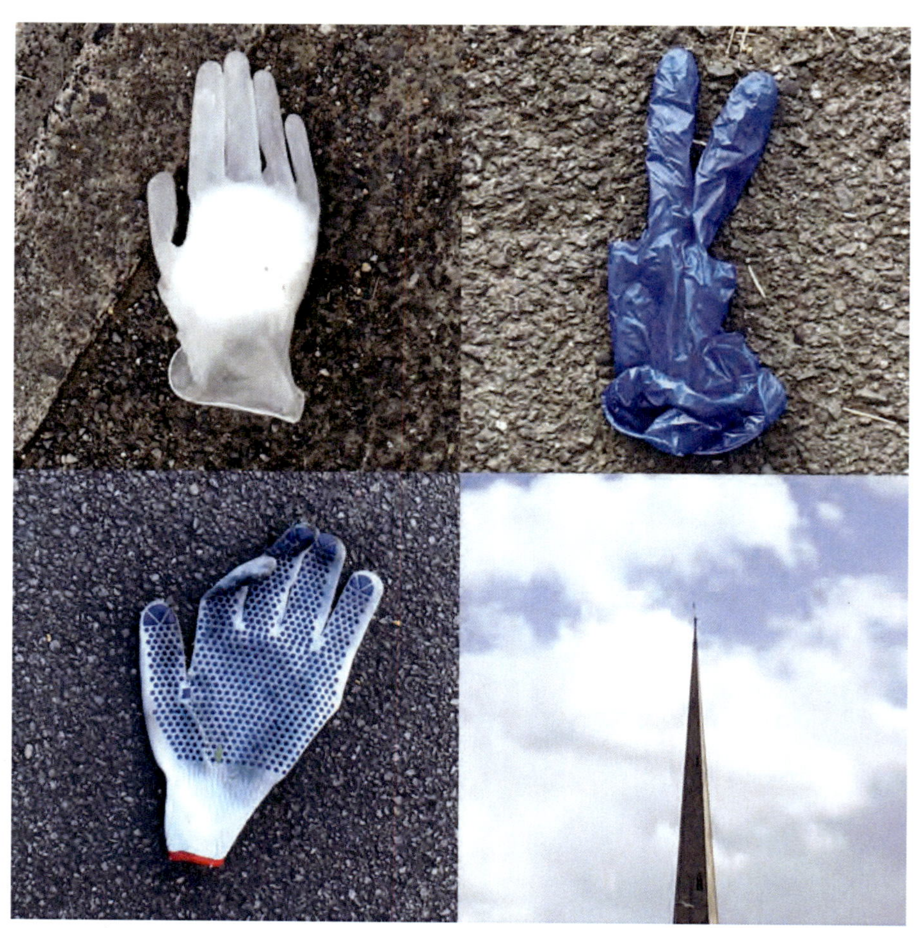

No.61 Glover's Needle

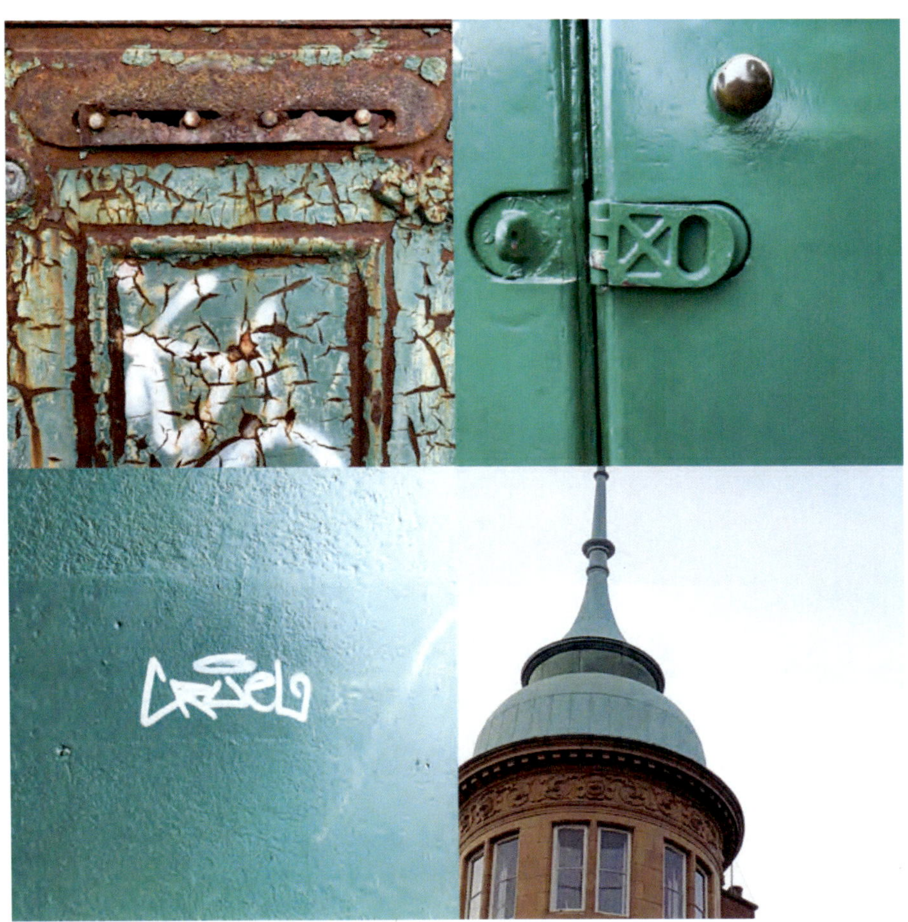

No.62 Turquoise

Conversations with Self in Lockdown

Penny Perrett

Talking to myself used to be something I did in my head...

After my partner died in 2018 I had regular conversations with him in my head and through a diary. Lockdown made me even more aware of my 'aloneness' and I started to talk to myself more regularly than I had done before. I consider myself a fit 'over 70' but I was suddenly viewed as 'old and vulnerable', and so not allowed to do the things that had become important to me in retirement, like work at the Foodbank and spend time with my grandchildren. By becoming my own conscience and my encouragement, I helped myself deal with this weird situation with humour, and from the comments of others, my conversations were duplicated in many of their own lives.

I spent most of my working life as a teacher, firstly in high schools teaching dance to high school students, and then with teachers. The power of dance to express creativity is unique. Without language, paint or pencil, we have only our bodies in space. Creating original movement to music has been another way for me personally to cope with difficult moments during the day. Although we could no longer work directly together, my dance group could film and share movement and so maintain that crucial contact with each other.

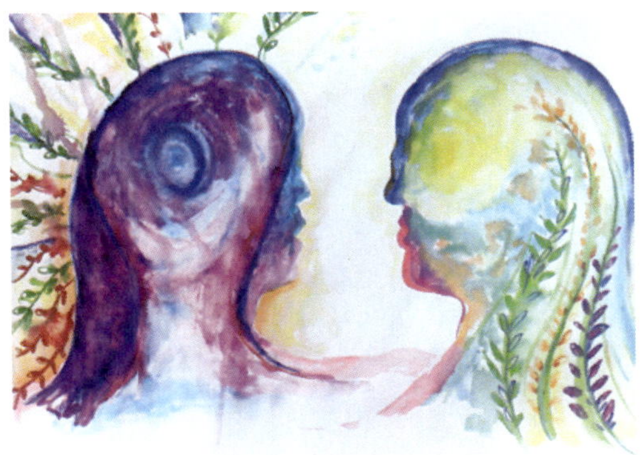

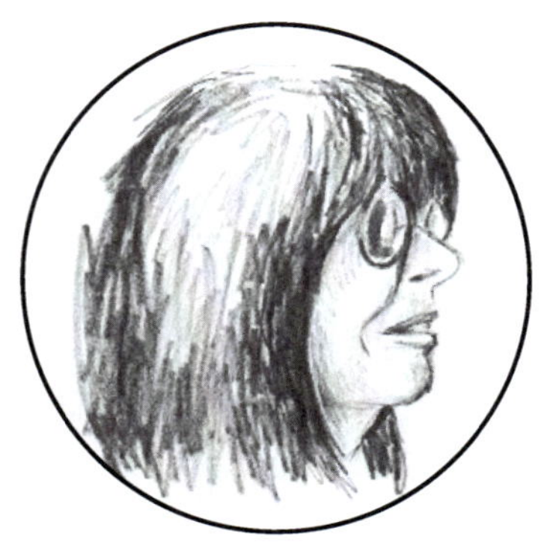

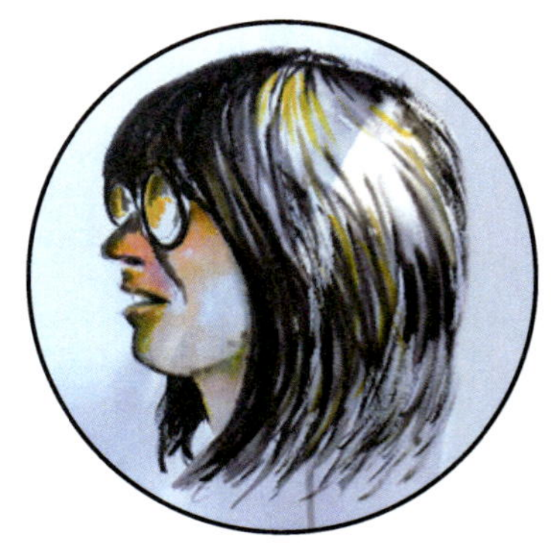

~ CONVERSATION 1 ~

I'm going to get up early and do my Pilates exercises.

You said that yesterday. Come on then.

Just 5 more minutes.

Bet you don't.

I will, just need to watch the news.

No news until 1pm you said.

OK. I think I'll have breakfast first.

If you have breakfast you'll not do the exercises.

OK. Tomorrow definitely. I will get up early.

Yea right....

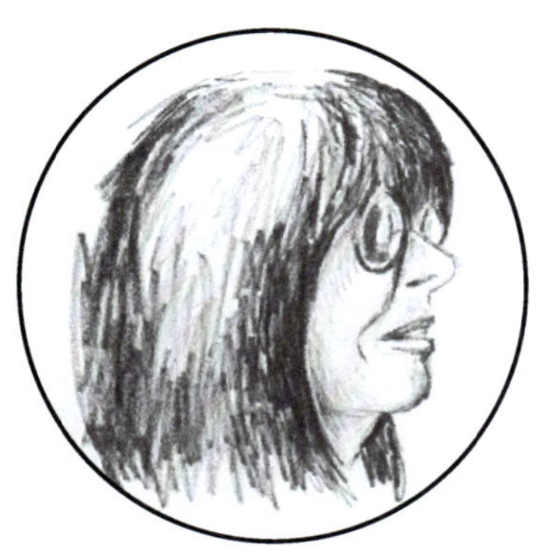

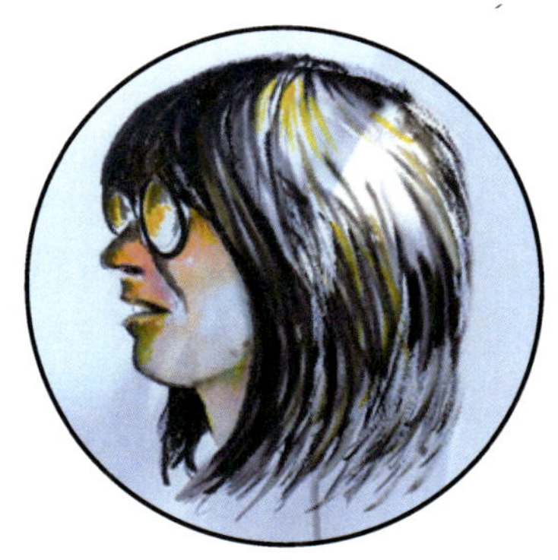

~ CONVERSATION 2 ~

Recycling day, there are lot of bottles in that bag?

No more than usual surely.

Certainly are.

Well I did finish a bottle of olive oil and balsamic vinegar... and the marmalade

Hmmm. And the rest?

The cider bottles are small.

Discipline required methinks.

Yea OK....

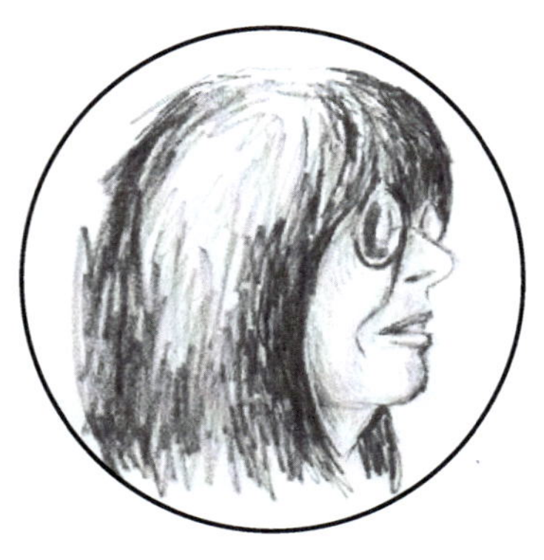

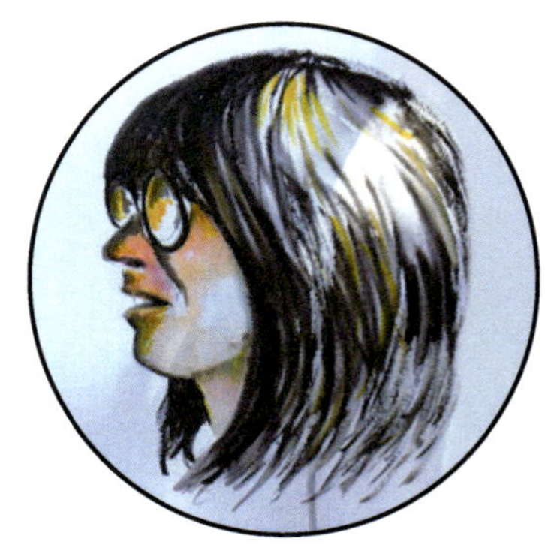

~ CONVERSATION 3 ~

I really fancy a biscuit.

You never buy biscuits.

I know but this is different.

So what are you going to do about it, you've just collected from the supermarket why didn't you order biscuits?

Because I never have biscuits.

So you need something sweet, what else is there?

Raisins. Dates. Satsumas.

Don't do it, though do they?

Maybe I could make some?

Yea right….

M&S have Easter Eggs half-price, mmmm

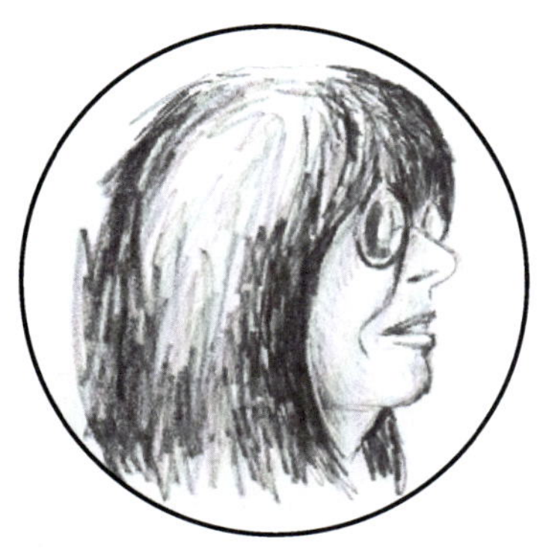

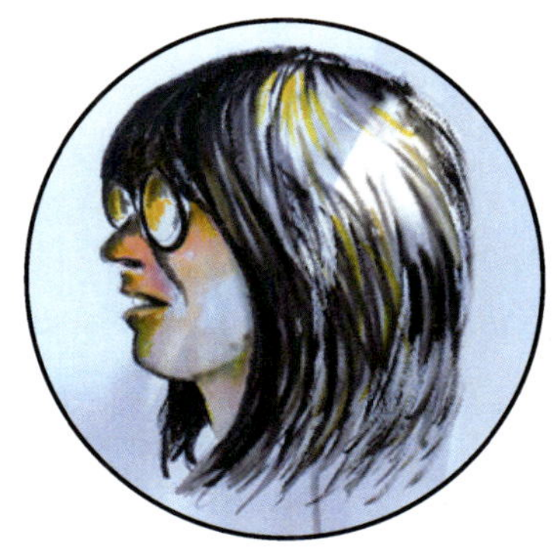

~ CONVERSATION 4 ~

I need a shower.

Well, have one.

Who is going to notice. I'm not likely to get up close and personal any time soon. If ever.

That is disgusting.

Legs need shaving.
Hair needs washing.

Well come on, sort yourself out. No-one is going to even want to get near you if you are smelly.

I'm not smelly.
But I will. Right now!

That's more positive...

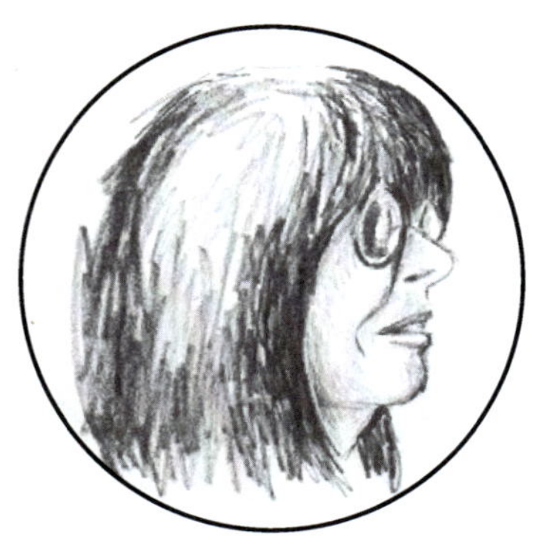

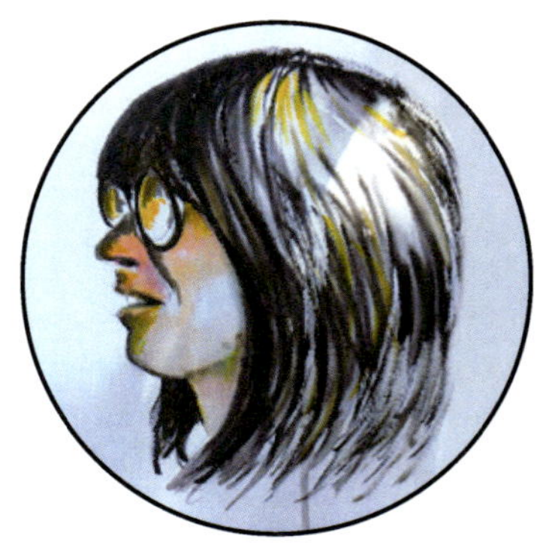

~ CONVERSATION 5 ~

It's 2am. Again.

Go to the loo quickly, you might go straight back to sleep

It's 3.30am. Definitely still awake. Again.

Do not put the radio on. Do not look at your phone. Make tea. Have a banana.

OK. I'll read for a bit.

No, you'll read the news. Listen to The Archers Omnibus podcast. That always works.

Did that yesterday. And the night before.

Did you get to the end?

No, fell asleep.

There you are, you can listen again…

zzzzzz….

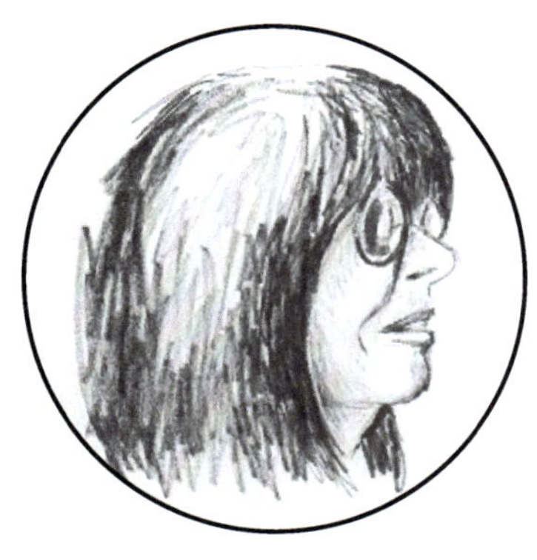

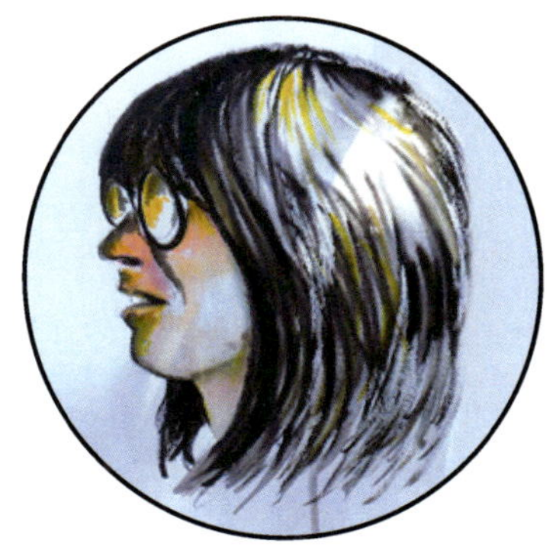

~ CONVERSATION 6 ~

Have you been on the scales?

Yep.

And?

Not lost a pound

Did you expect to?

Well I've done so much exercise since lockdown, I should've lost at least half a stone.

Think about it...

I am thinking. Muscle weighs more than fat, so that's probably why.

Walking and Pilates do not put on muscle.

And cycling. Maybe the scales are wrong.

You don't think the crisps might make a difference? And the ciders?

Tough times require treats.

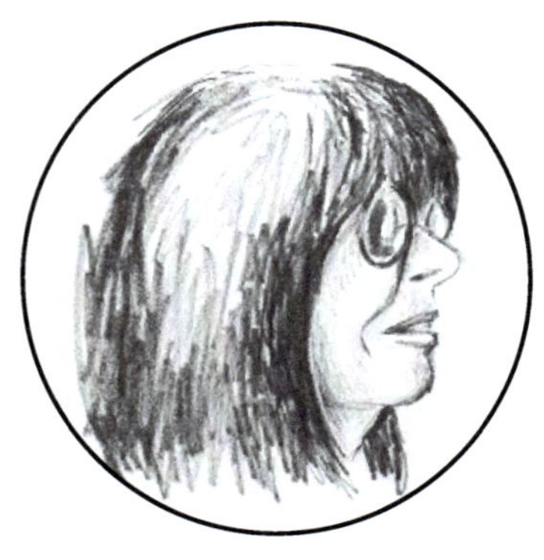

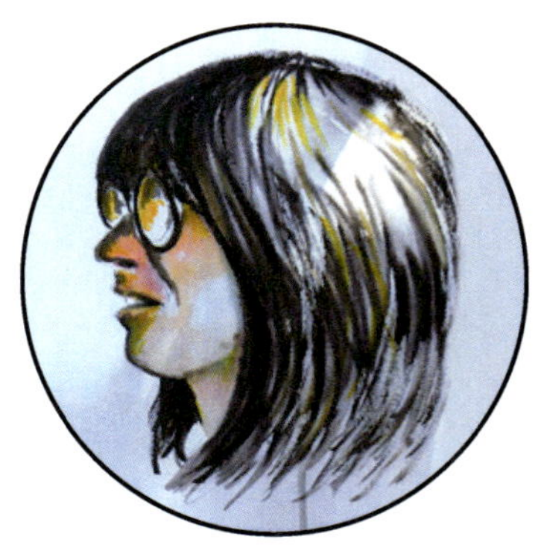

~ CONVERSATION 7 ~

Some good gardening going on. Do you know what you've planted?

I know roughly what I've planted, but not specifically where.

Why don't you use the little sticks and mark where you put things?

Because I think I will remember.

You don't remember anything else.

Anyway it makes it more of a surprise when things pop up.

Or don't.

Trouble is most of the seeds were 2 or 3 years old.

I don't think you'll be feeding yourself this year then.

The kale will grow, it always does. And the radishes.

Yum-yum...

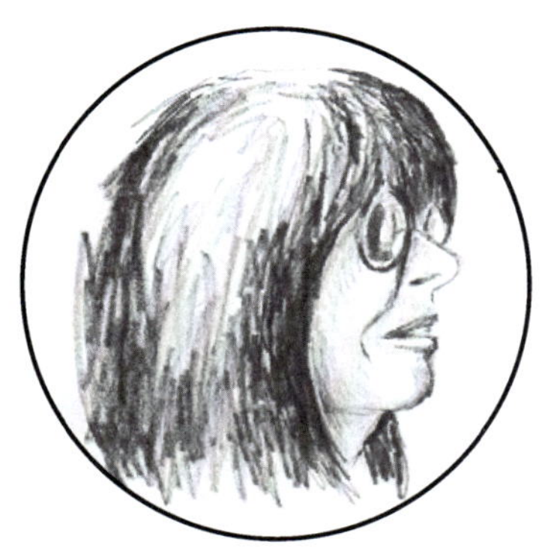

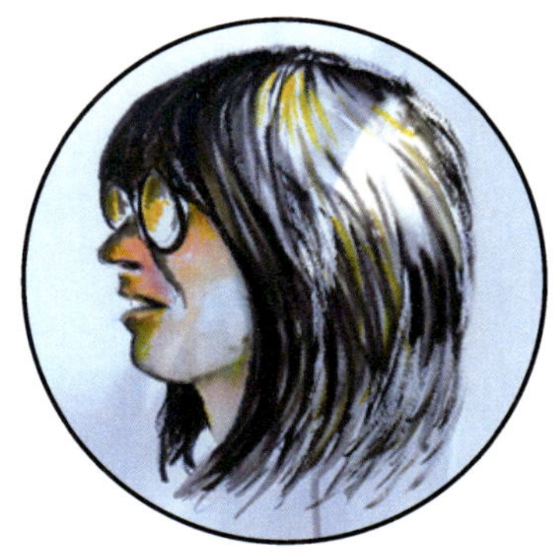

~ CONVERSATION 8 ~

I really need some cheese.

Supermarket pick-up in a couple of days, can't you wait?

I'll pop into M&S, it's super quiet there and it's early.

In your PJs?

They're tracky bottoms not PJs.

You wear them as PJs.

They're not PJs though.

And no bra.

Does anyone care? People are so concerned about keeping their distance they don't notice anyone else anyway.

Your mother would say that you are letting yourself go.

The freedom is wonderful, l rarely wore a bra in the 70s...

Not sure that's a good comparison.

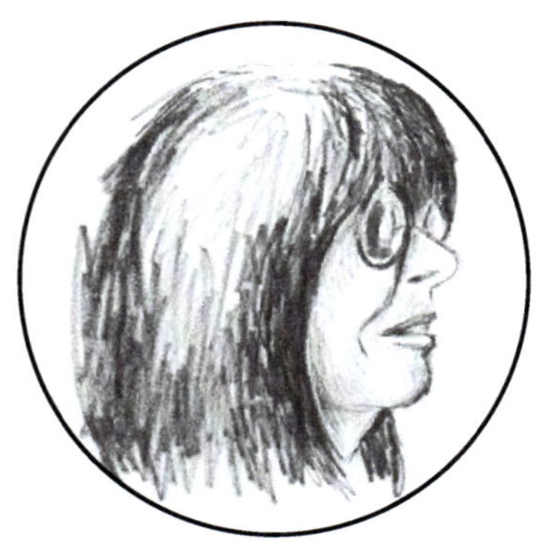

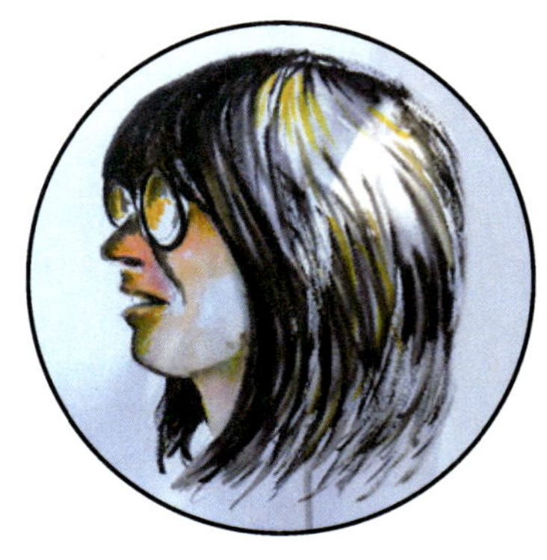

~ CONVERSATION 9 ~

Decision making is really hard.

More so than usual?

No, I always find it difficult to make decisions.

So what's different?

Decisions used to be about big things. Money.Holidays.Jobs.

And now?

Well, there's the jigsaw decision which is ongoing. And whether to do the long walk, the short walk or the medium walk.

That depends surely on your energy and the weather?

Marmite or marmalade on my toast.

Have both.

Facetime or WhatsApp? Dishwasher or wash up by hand? Comfy knickers or sexy knickers?

FFS.

Second G&T or glass of wine?

Water will mean better sleep.

I'm not asking for actual advice. Just to support my choices.

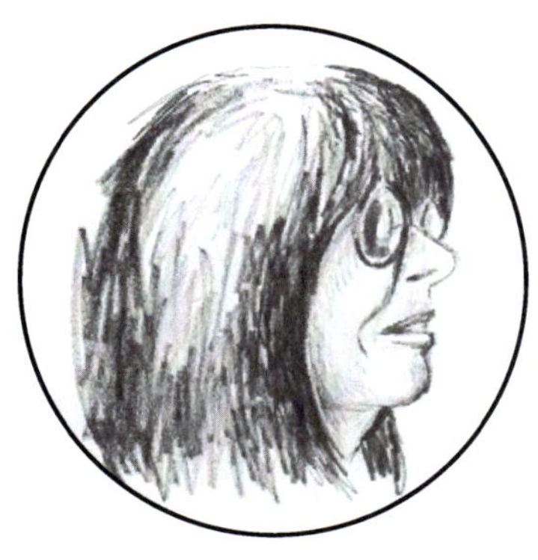

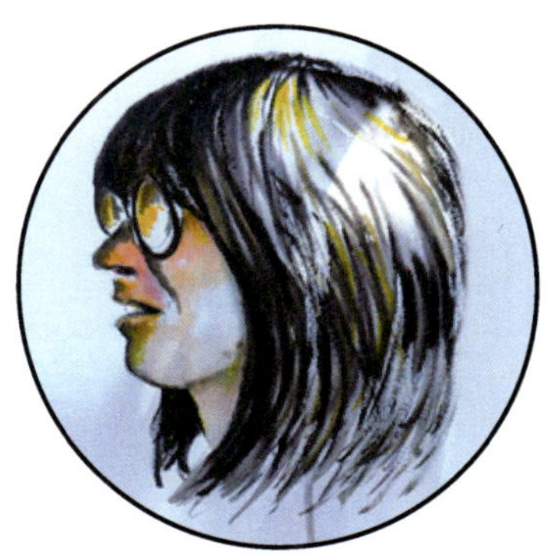

~ CONVERSATION 10 ~

People are learning a new language, writing books and painting masterpieces during lockdown, so impressive...

So, what are you doing?

It's so hard to concentrate on anything, I drift from one thing to another.

What do you want to do?

I'd like to learn the names of the trees in the park, identify the songs of the birds in the garden, open the piano lid and my sketch book, read something other than the paper.

Not much then. So, what have you done so far today?

Walked. Discovered some new bits of Worcester. Talked to 2 strangers. Put 6 pieces into the hardest jigsaw ever. Washed the sheets. Watched the bread rising.

Be kind to yourself. There's always tomorrow....

Elle 1:1000000

Sara Hayward

I began the Elle 1:1000000 series of figurative paintings in January 2020 celebrating the energy of the female form and the vitality and inner strength of women around the world. Working on multiple images I work through a series of images simultaneously to retain freshness and immediacy using fast-drying acrylic paints to allow the layers to build. I like to use a limited palette and incorporate printmaking techniques into the paintings. Many of the images came from newspaper cuttings found during lockdown.

Painting during the crisis felt very poignant: whilst I had more time to paint, I missed social interaction and mourned our former life. We all began to wonder what the "new" normal of the future would look like. Painting daily was an important distraction for me as the gravity of events unfolded: working sometimes at dawn and sometimes at midnight, the series completely enveloped me.

During the spring I was inspired by photographs of a memory blanket knitted by my friend on the coast and decided to create my own version in bold, vibrant colours. I tried to knit a square every evening and found it both meditative and calming during the crisis. I enjoyed the way the colours both clashed and complemented each other, reminding me of some of my favourite artists. I also liked the way the squares knitted together as I went along. Three other members of our household have caught the knitting bug and begun memory blankets too, so be warned, memory blankets are highly contagious and addictive! As the crisis developed my blanket grew and comforted me in the evenings as I watched the news.

Sara Hayward

Sara Hayward is an artist living and working in Worcester. She studied fine art at the Ruskin School of Drawing & Fine Art, Oxford University, and printmaking at the Royal College of Art, London. Sara's semi-abstract, expressive, painterly style is concerned with capturing the energy of her subject matter using a heightened colour palette and printmaking inspired mark-making techniques. She is married to the landscape painter Paul Powis and they live and work together in Battenhall.

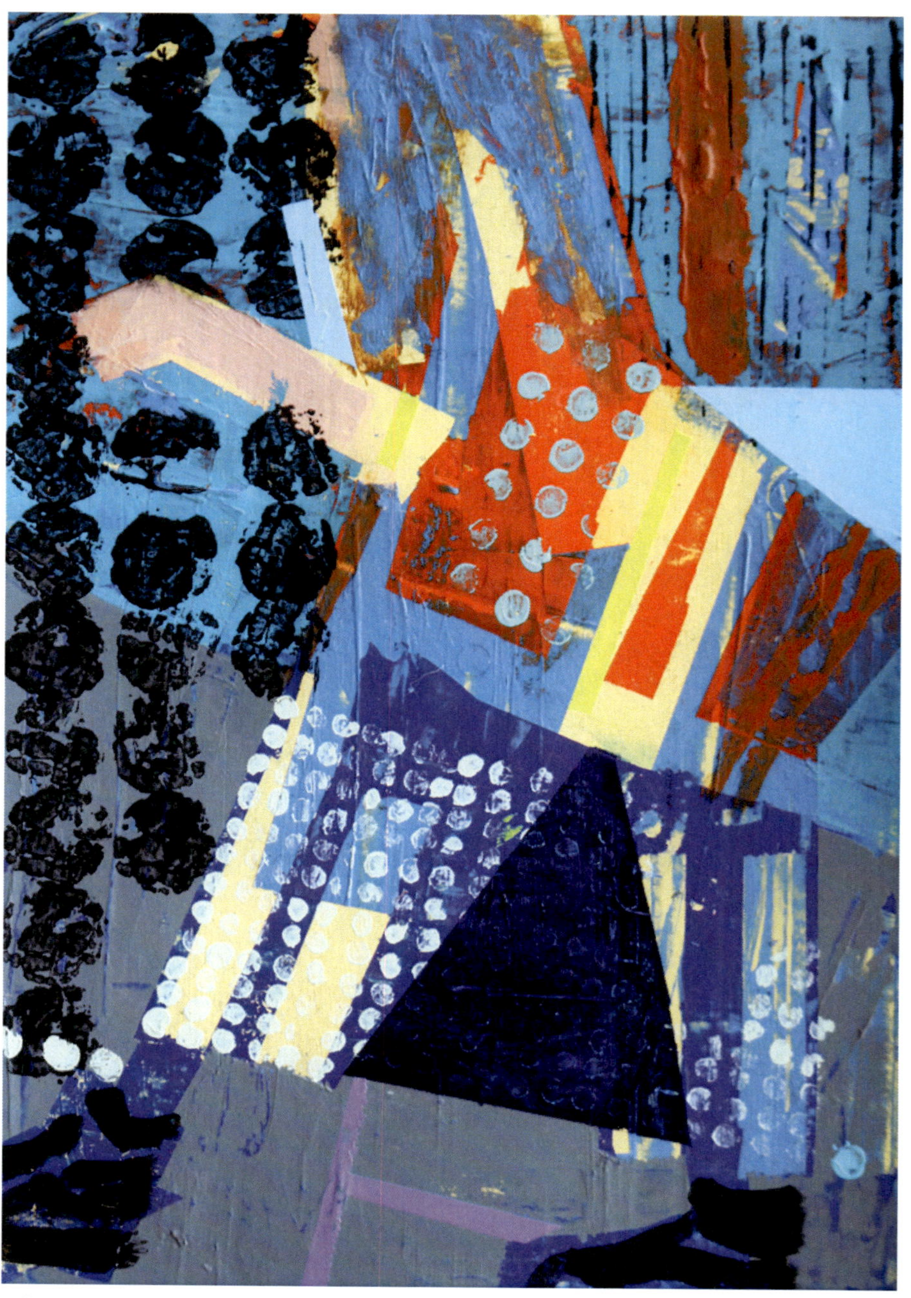

Elle#28

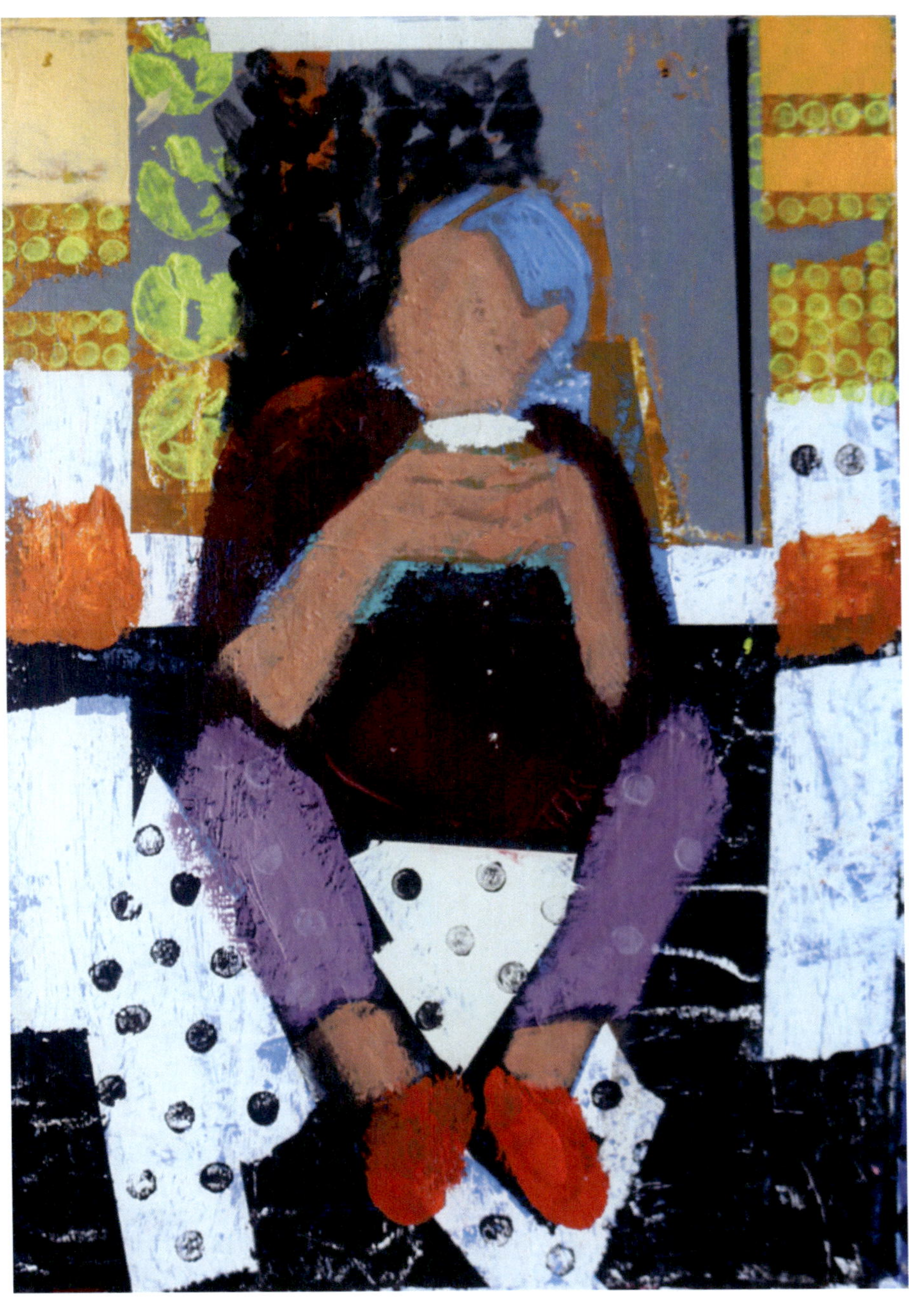

Elle#27

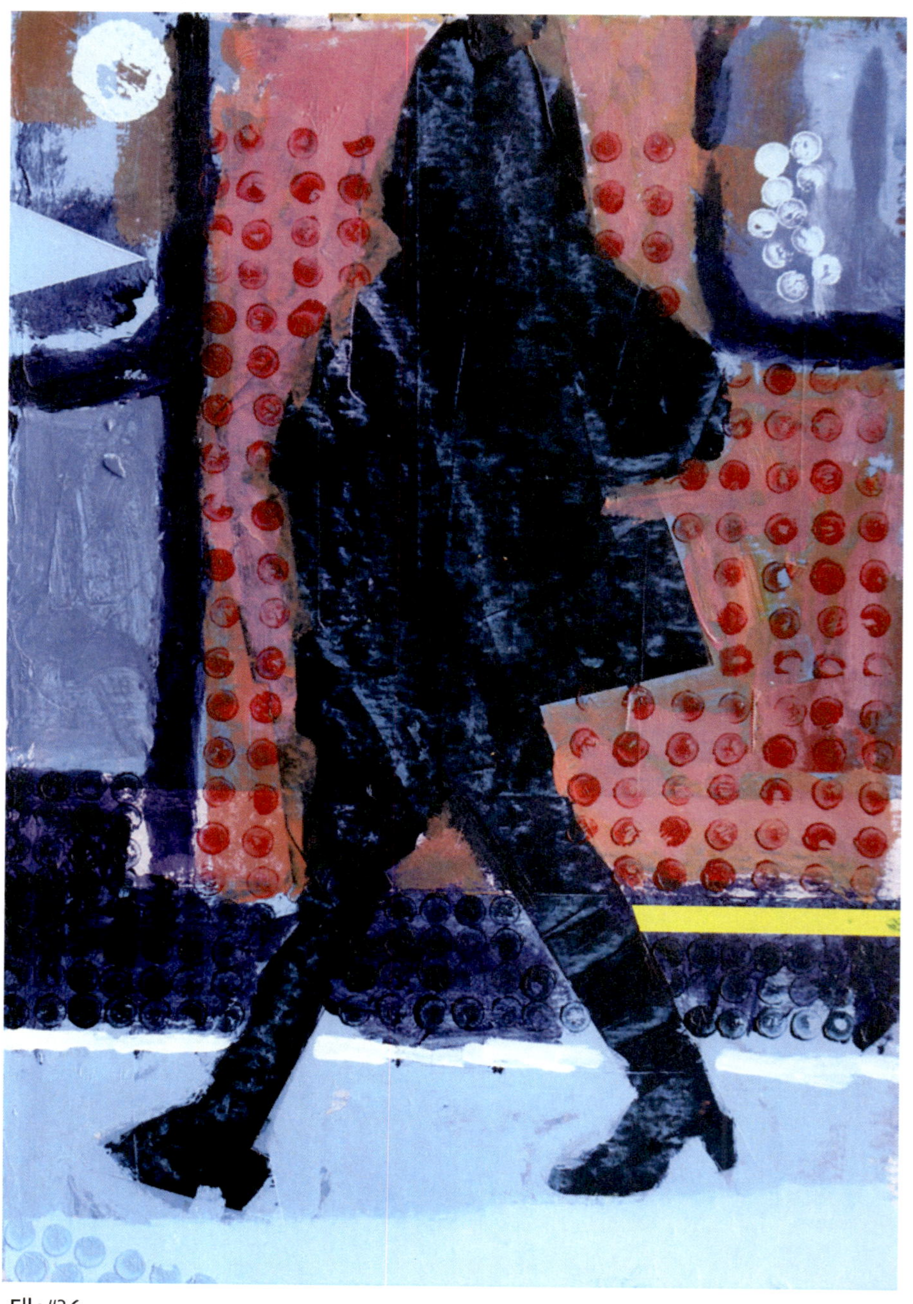

Elle#36

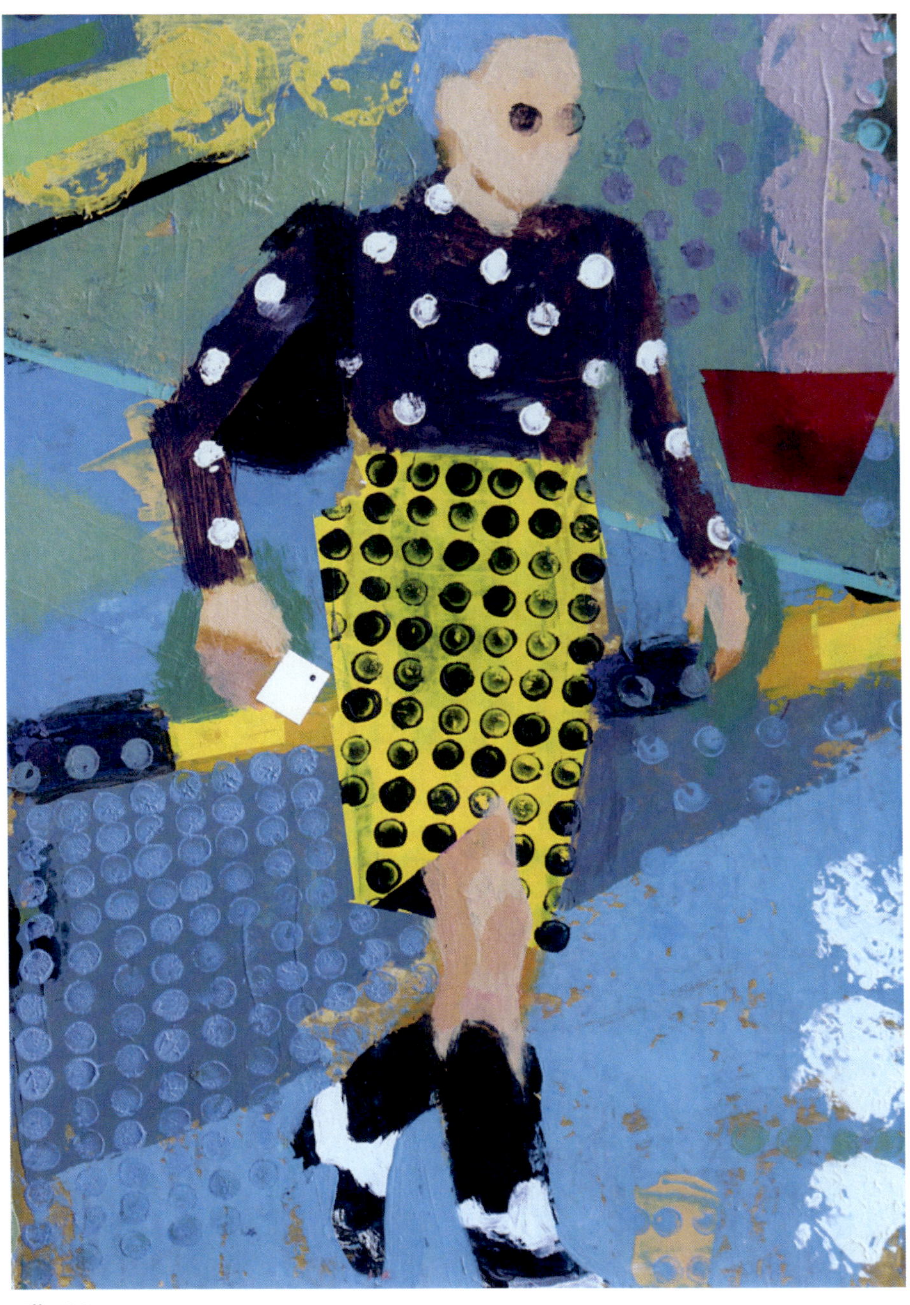

Elle#39

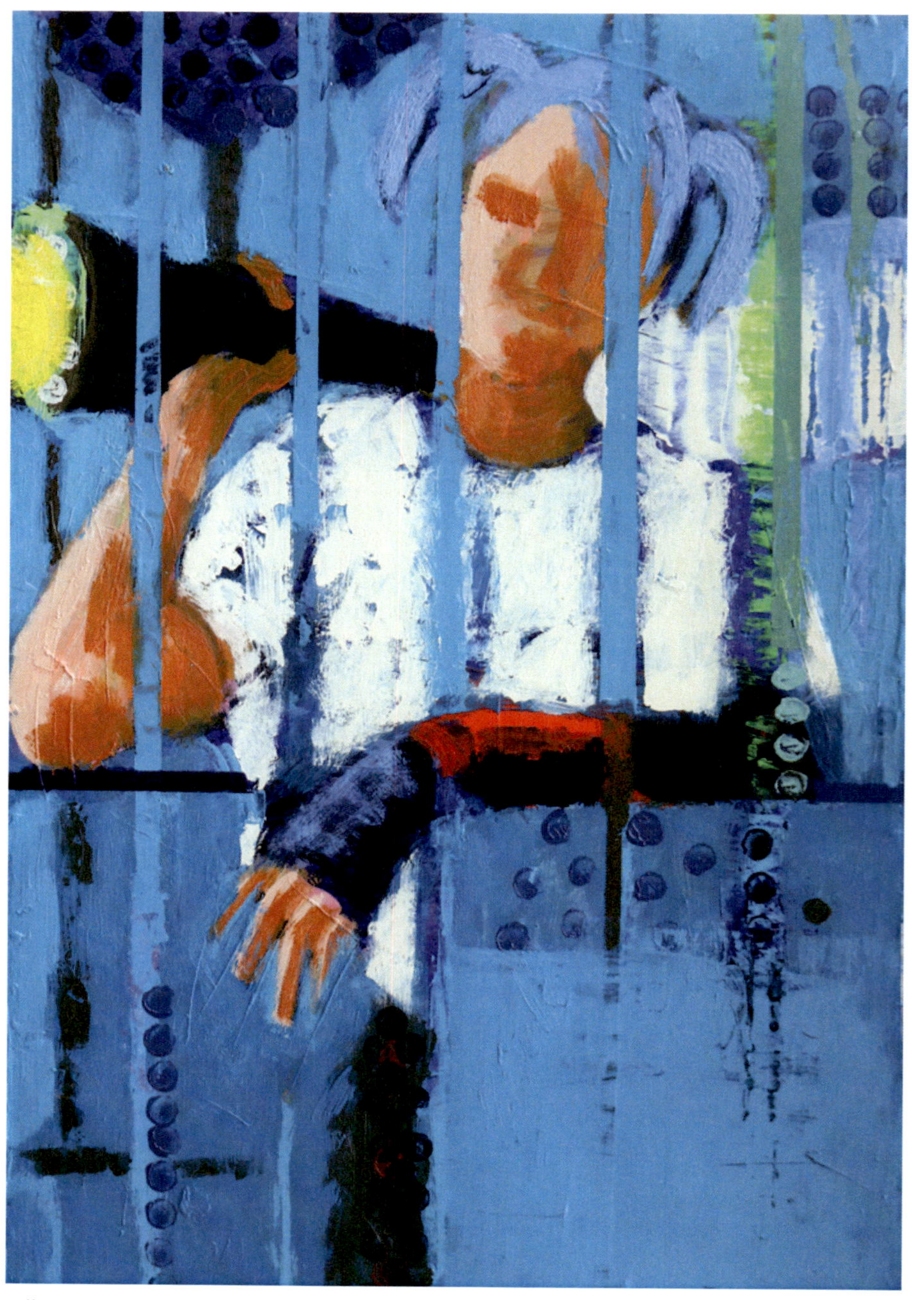

Elle#47

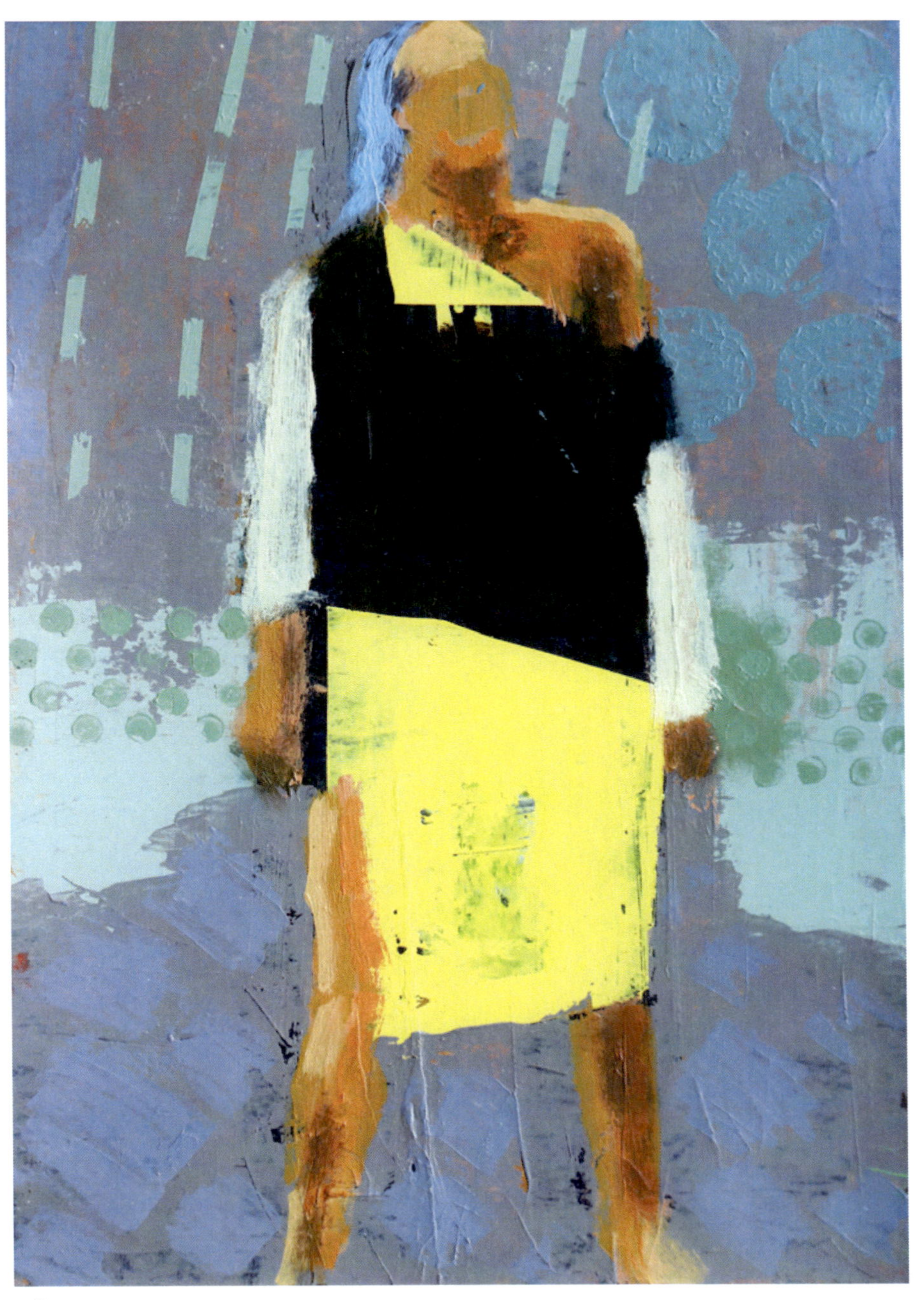

Elle#50

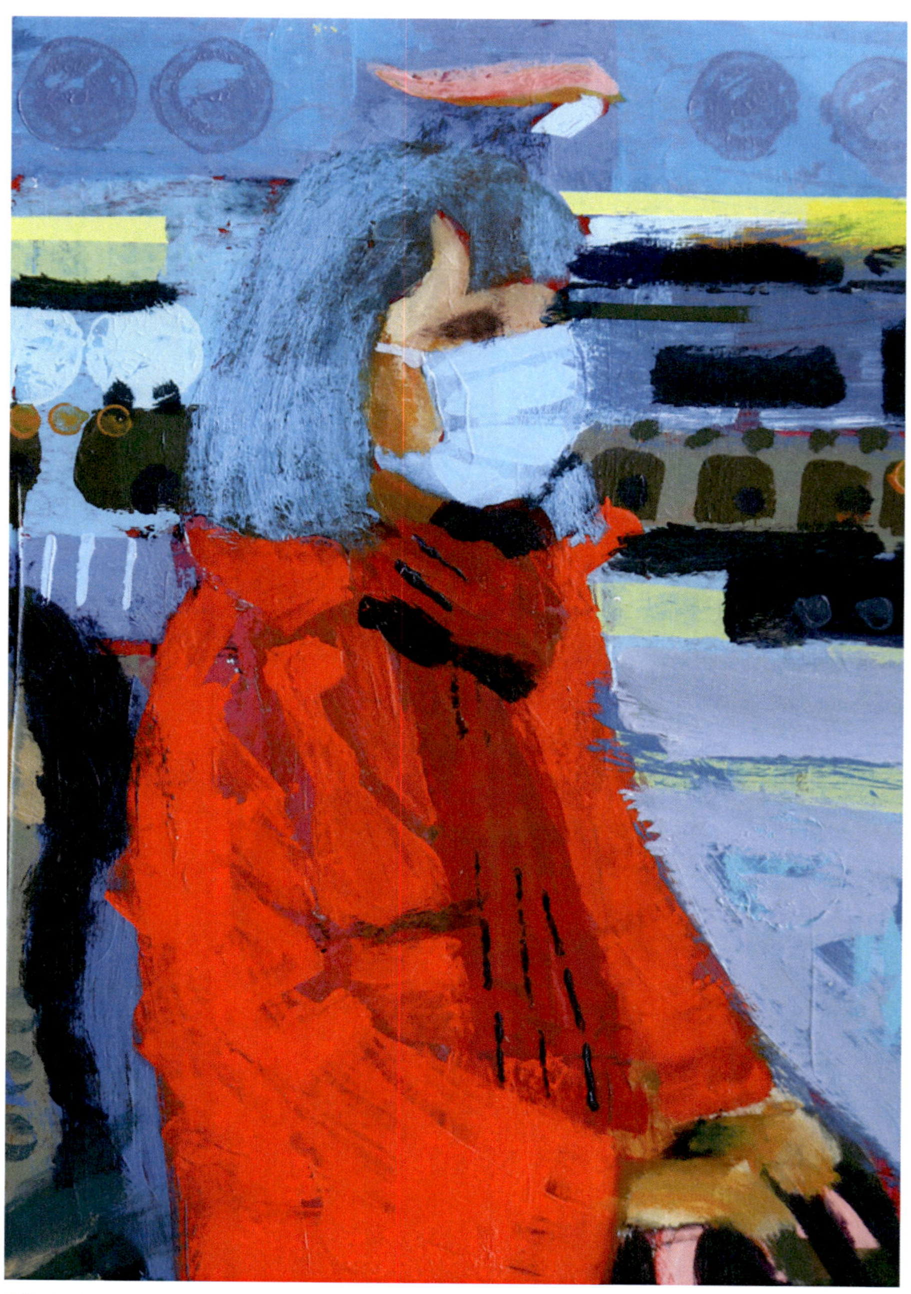

Elle#62

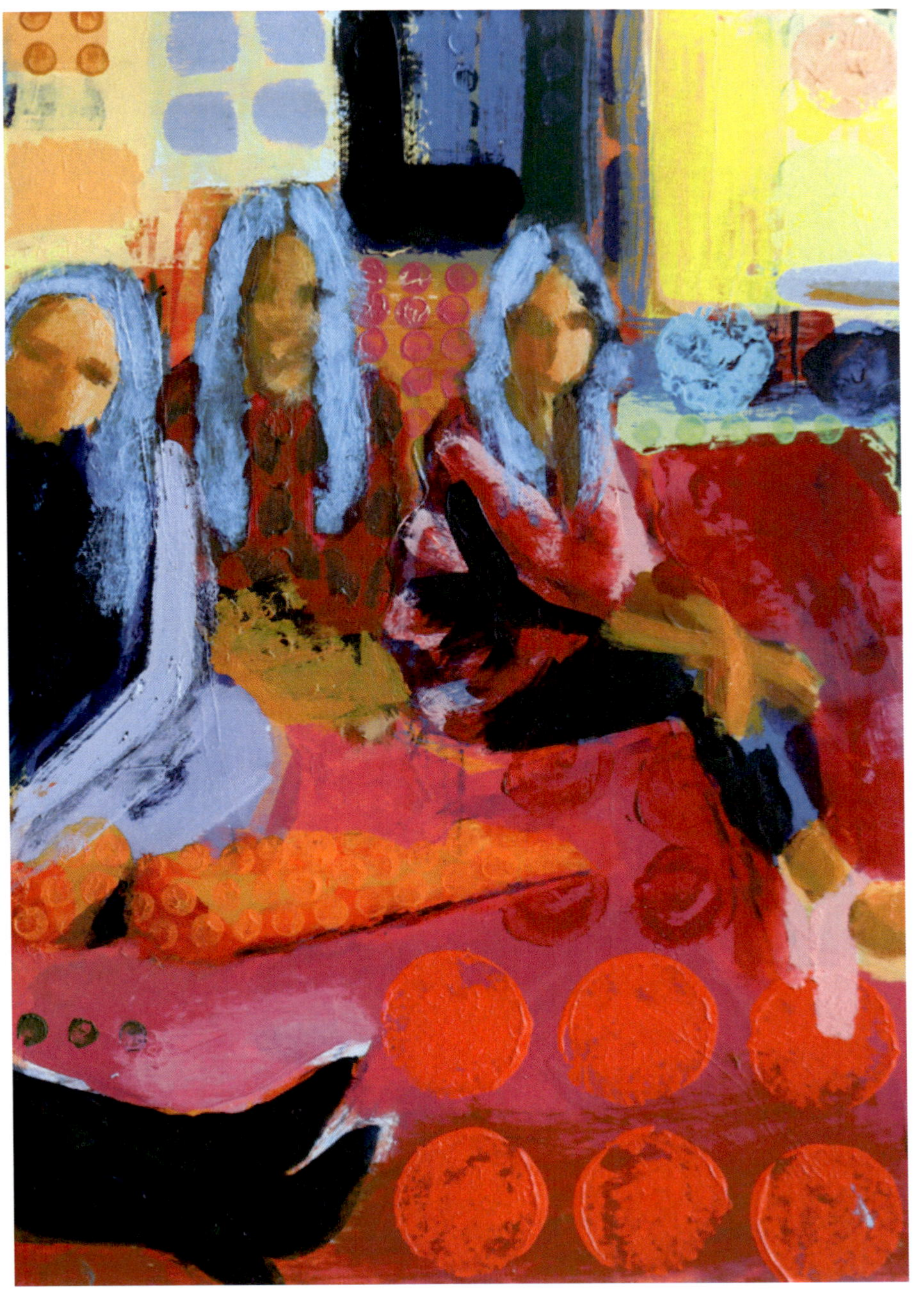

Elle#64

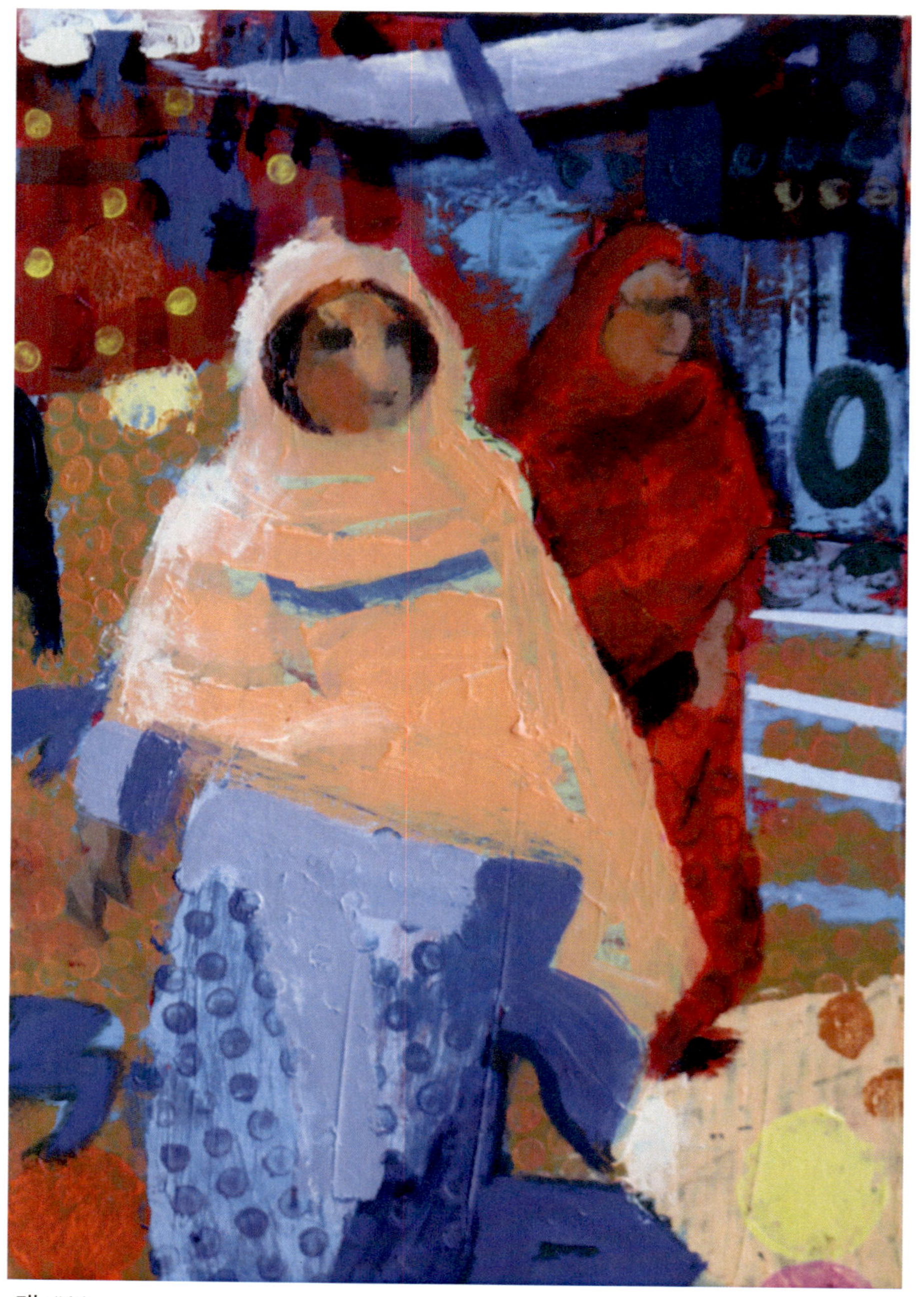

Elle#66

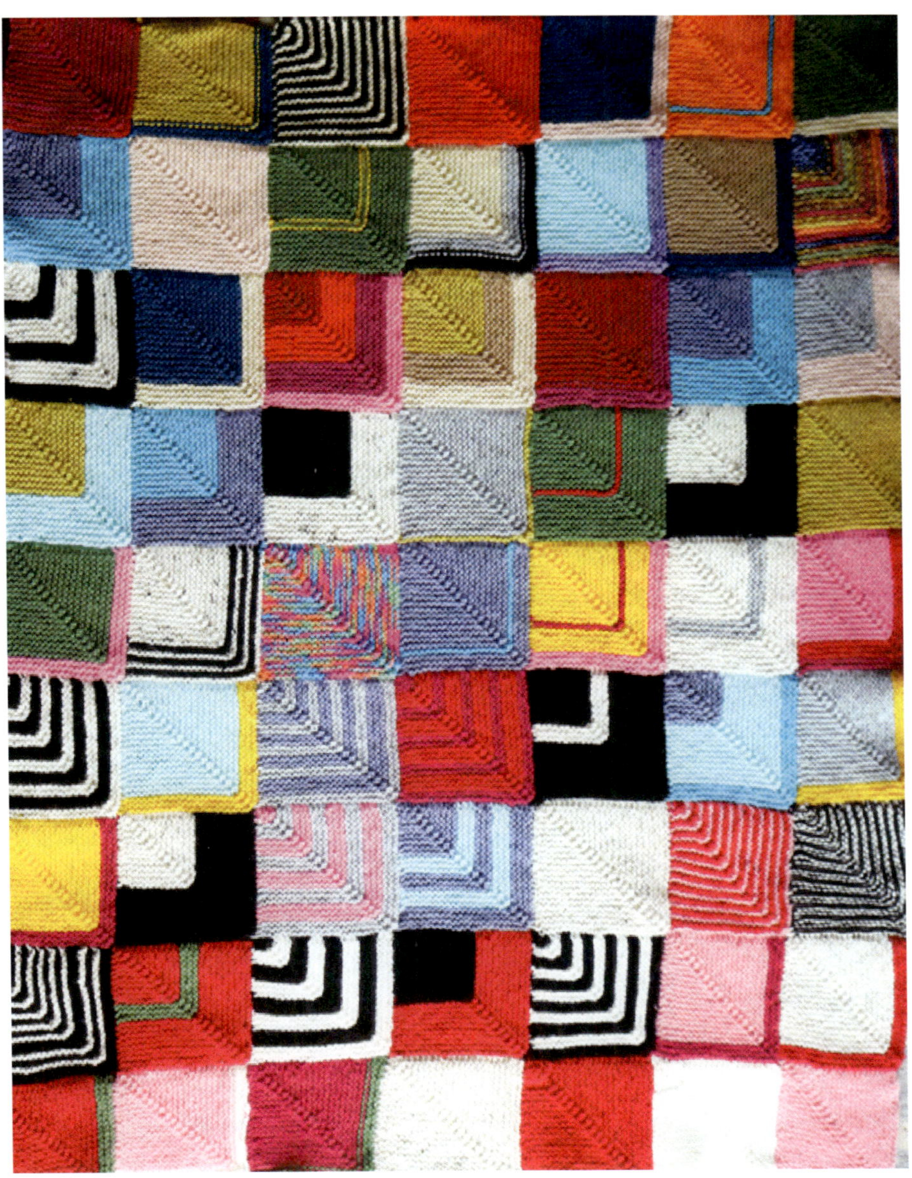

Memory Blanket

Don't Panic!

Sarah Ling

Usually, life foxtrots at a pace so fast, so frantic, it's easy to run out of time to do the things you love. There's dinner to make, uniform to wash, emails to answer; there's the choreography of getting the children to and from school, with a pack-up that won't make them wince, with clean socks and a shirt free from sauce. There's your own commute, then planning and teaching and checking and marking; there're the endless internal questions: have we got enough milk? Does the cat have fleas? Did I hand those essays back? What if I catch Covid and pass it on?

For me and my family lock down was kind. We're fortunate to have a garden, and the weather was beautiful. My husband and I kept our jobs: gardening for him, teaching for me. The frantic dance of life was still there, sometimes more so on my

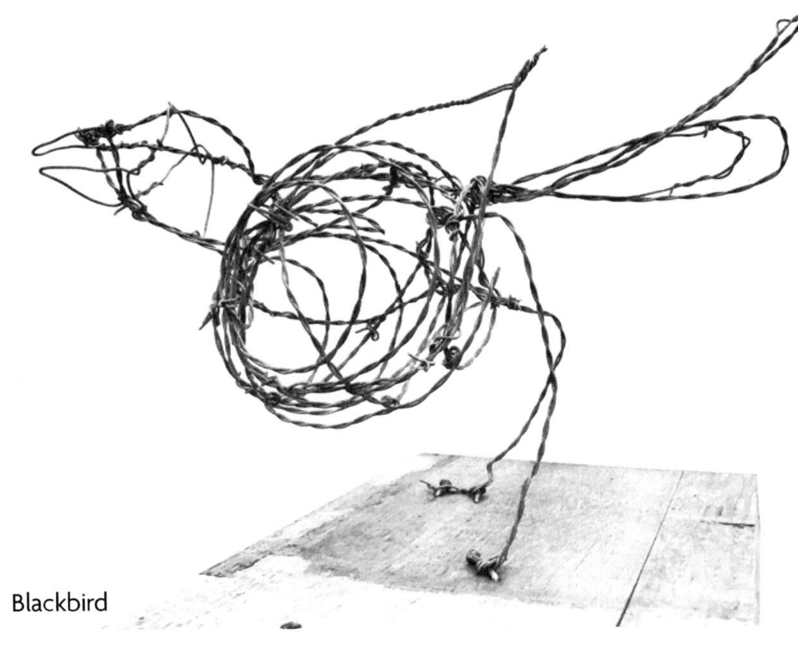

Blackbird

working days: my two children and I sharing the laptop as they stumbled through their school work and I attempted virtual teaching: video lessons, meetings by Zoom, marking formative assessments without a pen or book in sight, everything centred around the screen. And all the while, ever-conscious of the growing threat of coronavirus; all the while, juggling priorities: on-line school work versus mental health; literacy comprehension versus reading a book in the garden; computer maths versus a game of monopoly: practising spellings versus playing on the swings.

My internal barrage of questions began to include: Does it really matter if this assignment never gets completed? When will the robust testing system be properly up and running? How is our death rate so high? Why do I keep hearing more about the economy than our nation's health?

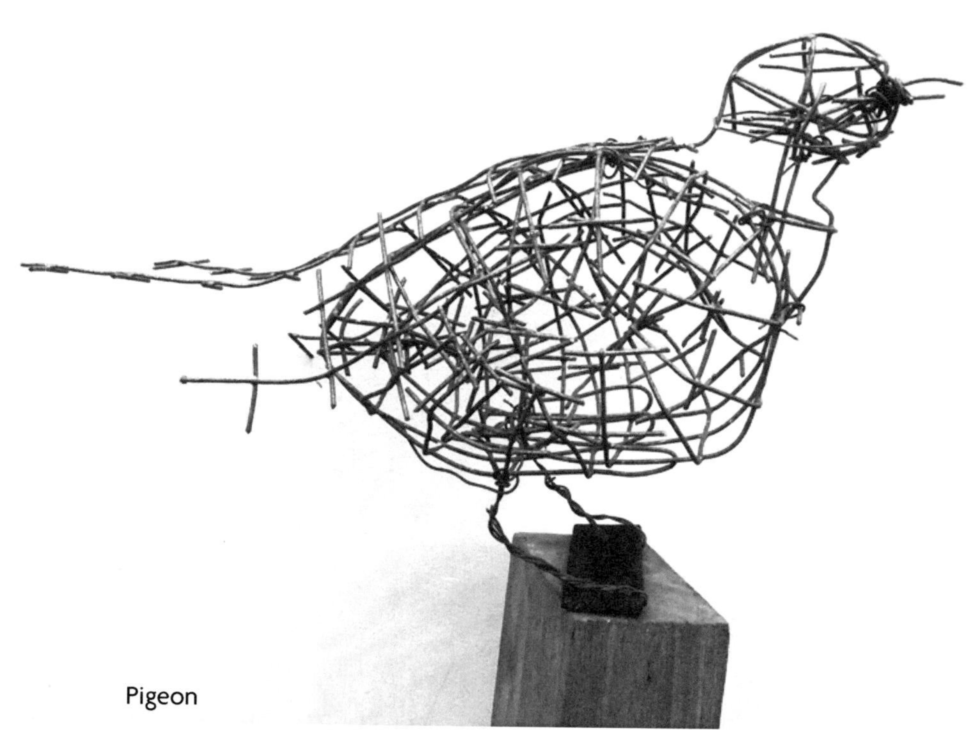

Pigeon

I deliberately made my days off a slow, gentle waltz. We weren't allowed to be anywhere; we didn't have to keep time. Covid made us full of care, and gave us time to stand and stare. The kids and I lost ourselves: drawing, reading, writing in the garden. Boredom allowed our imaginations to grow, so we used what we had – crayons, coloured pencils, oil pastels, paint, left-over wire mesh from the depths of the shed. I love how drawing absorbs: I love how mistakes sometimes make a picture better. It was wonderful to lose myself in seeing and making, and to have something tangible at the end.

I'm determined that our new normal won't be business as usual. Often we will slow the frantic foxtrot of life, and often, we will halt it altogether: I'll waltz the wire through the air, pirouette the paint across the canvas, invite the eye and the hand to partner up with the pencil and move, free-form, across the page.

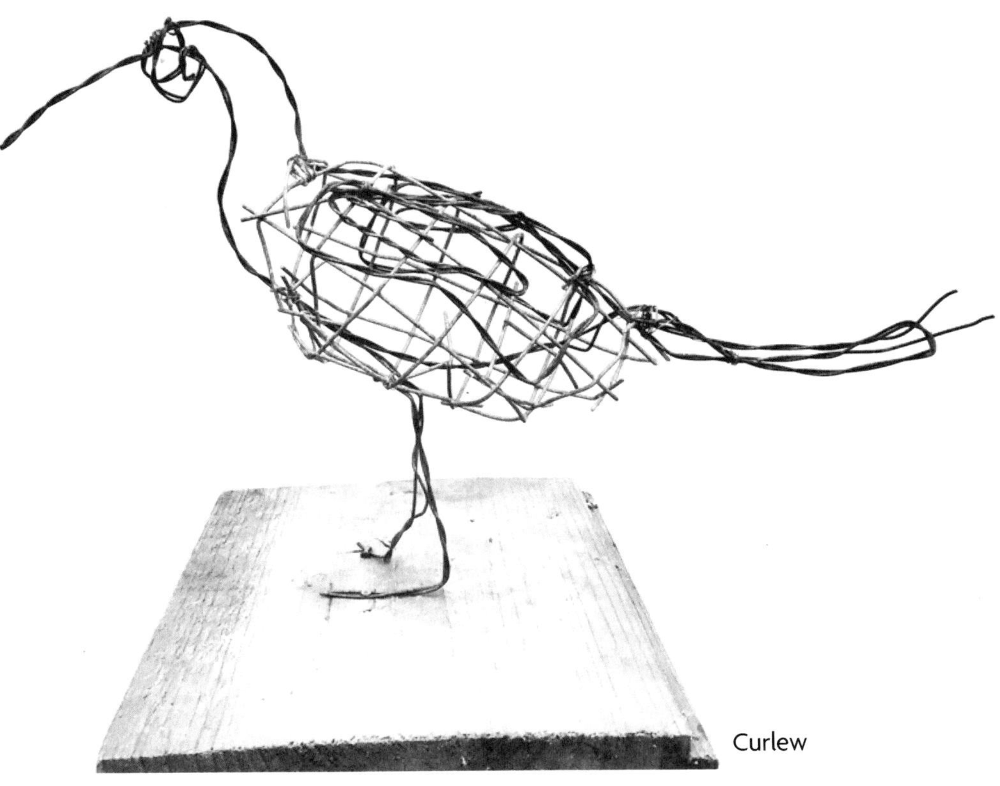

Curlew

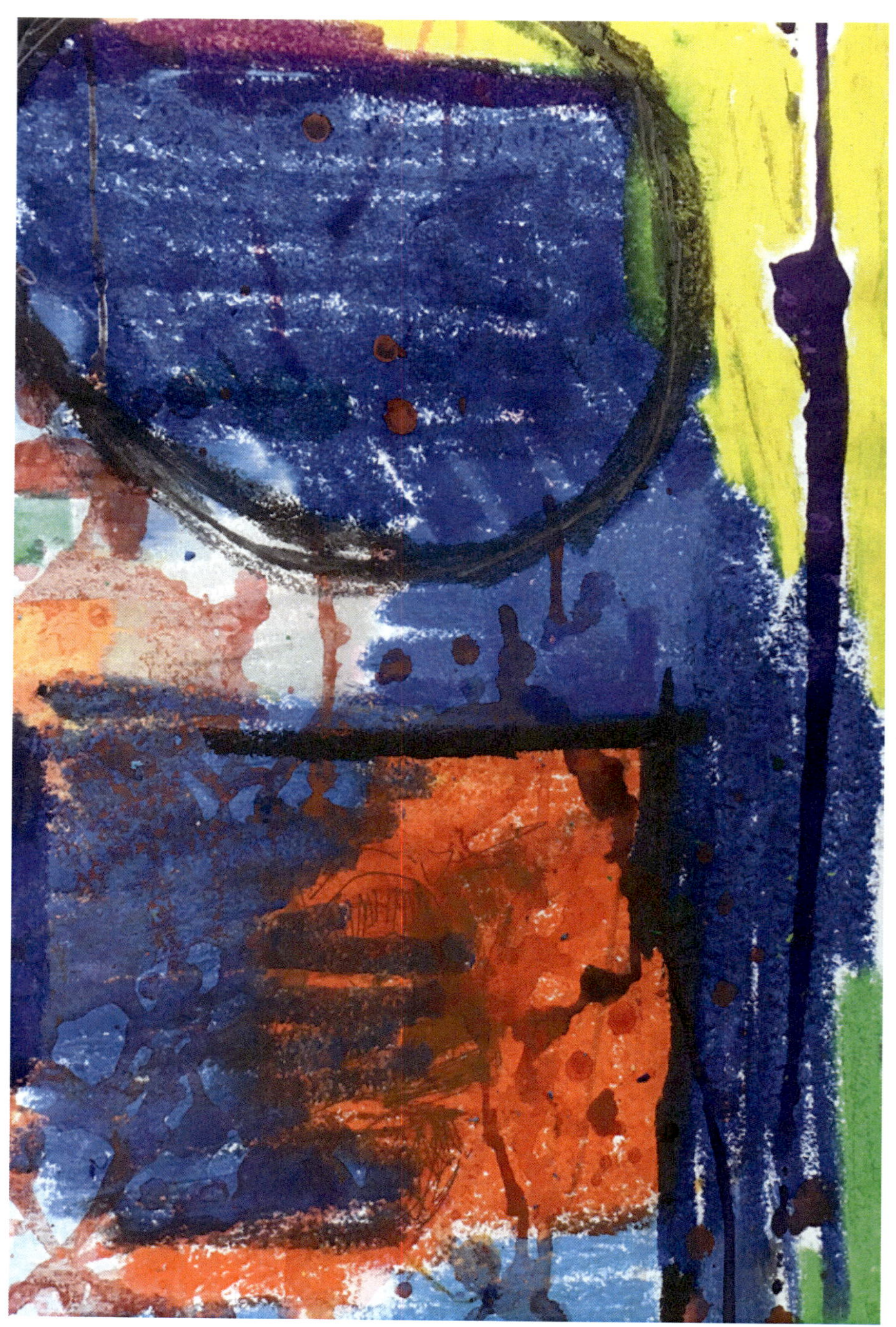

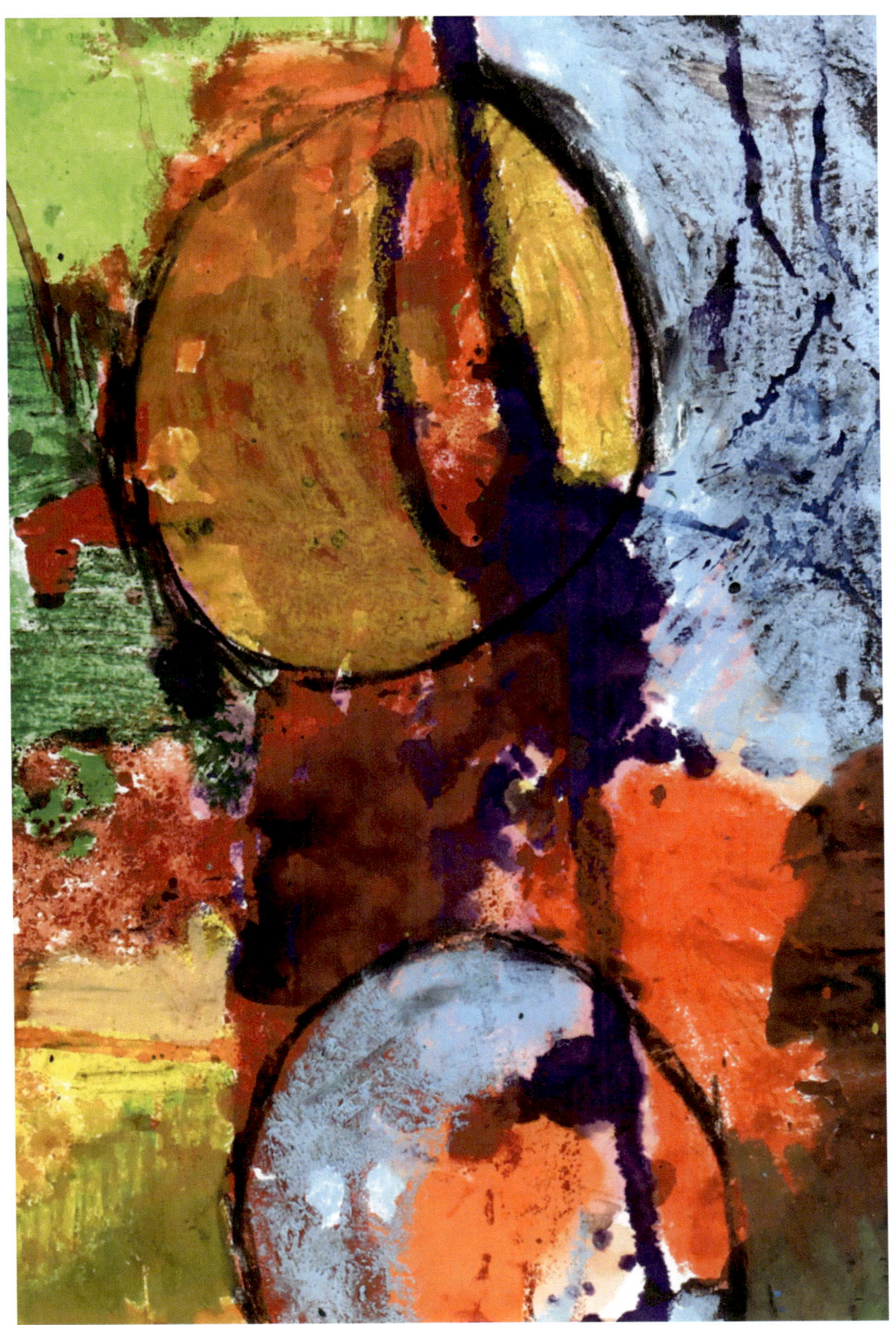

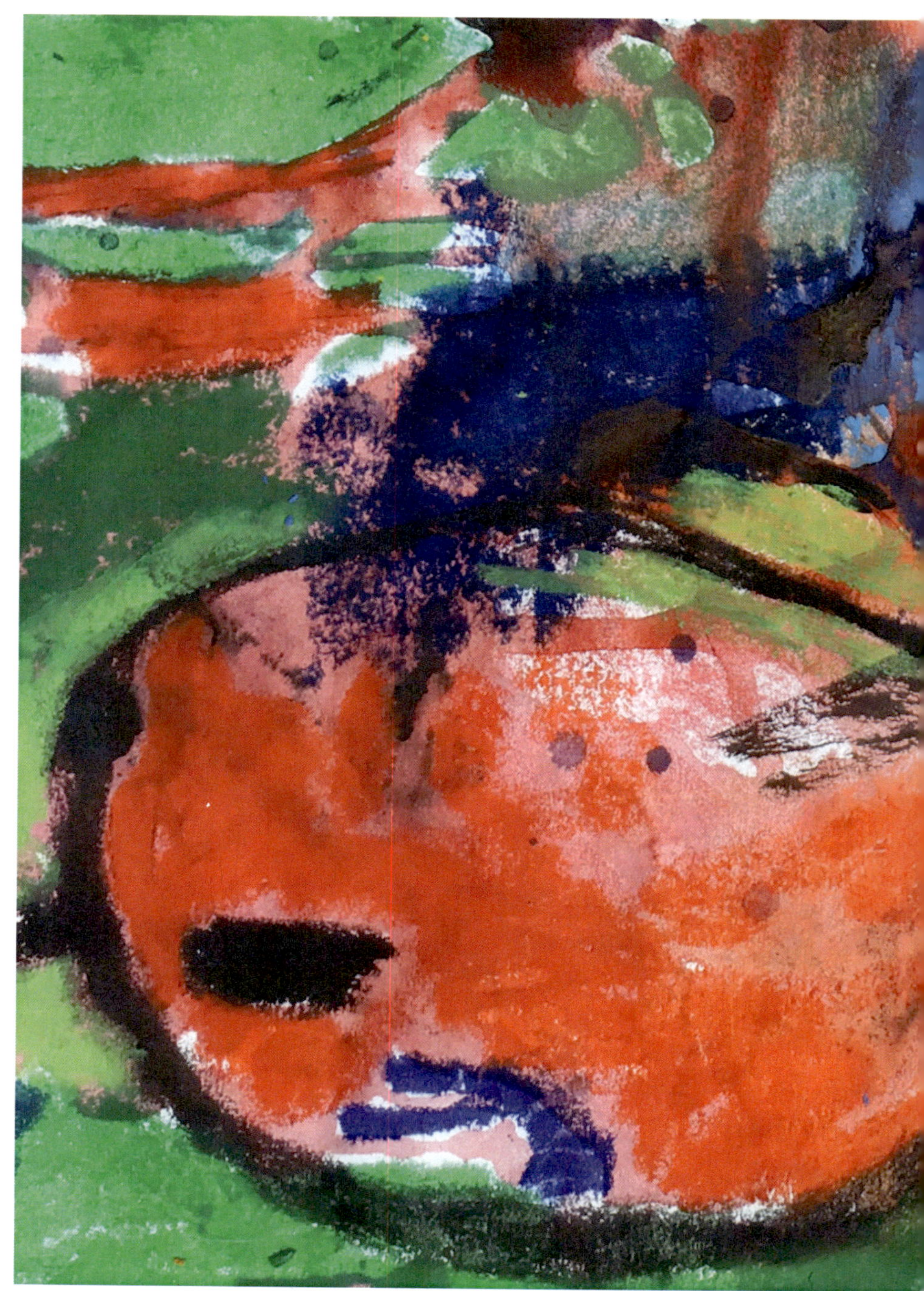

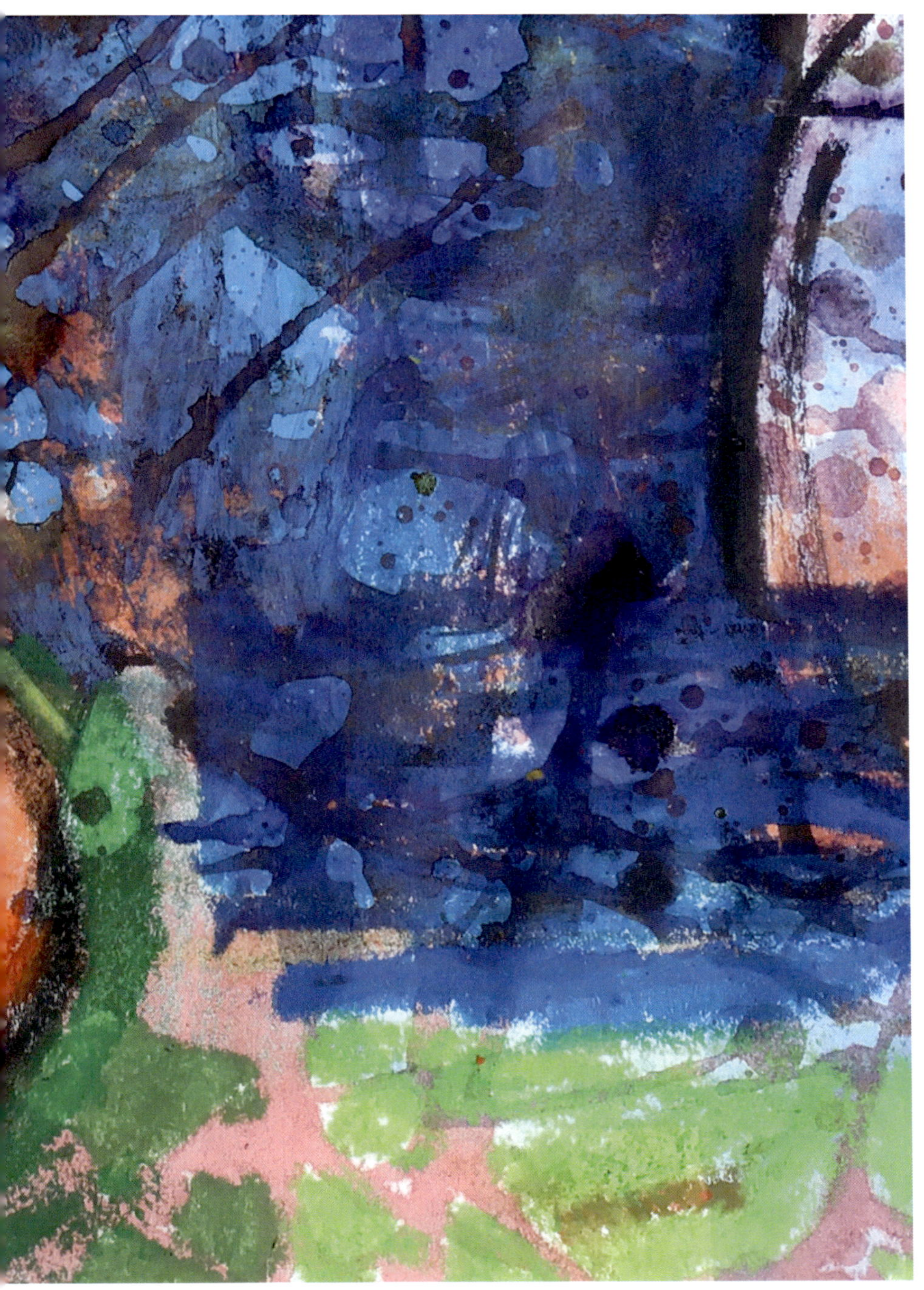

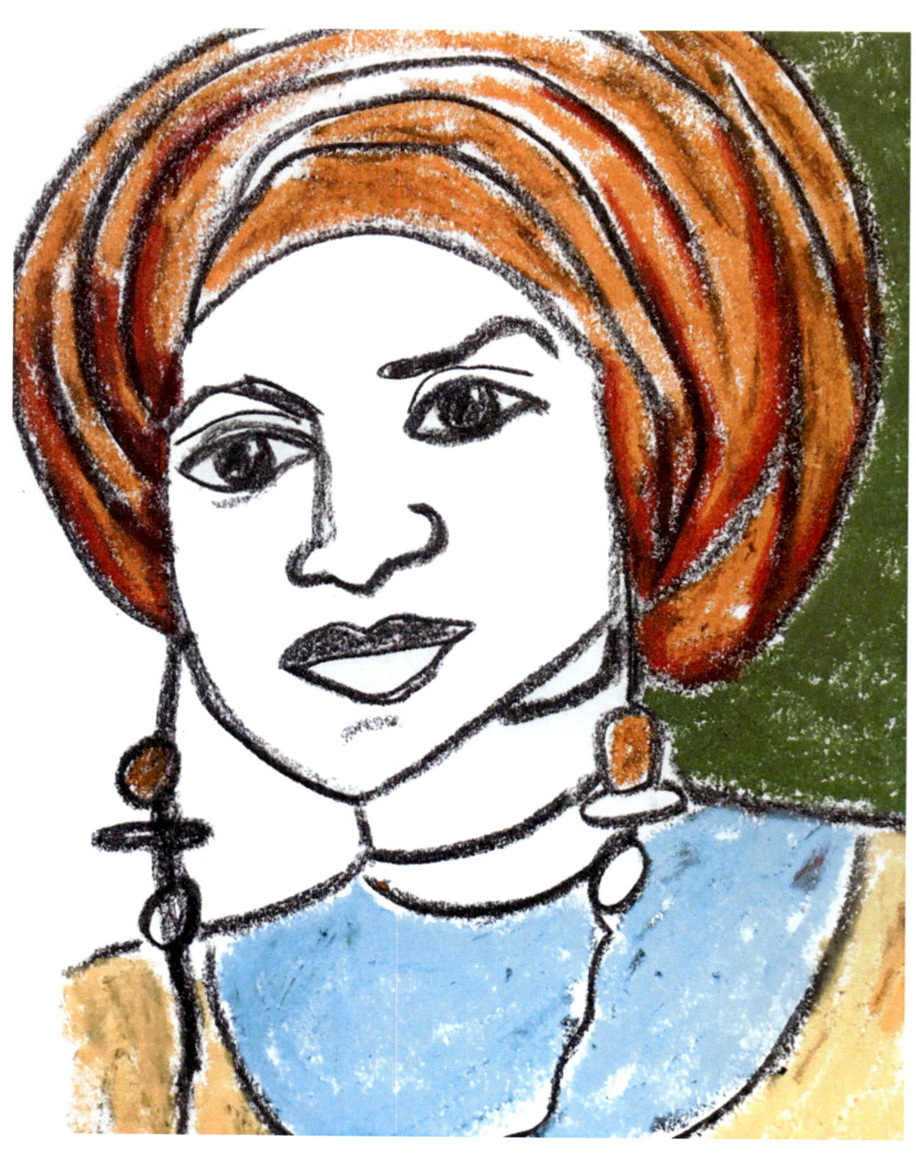

Joining an online life-drawing and portraiture club gave me much needed regular, structured practice and feedback. I haven't drawn so much since my art degree, and I enjoyed it immensely – one of the real positives to emerge during lock-down.

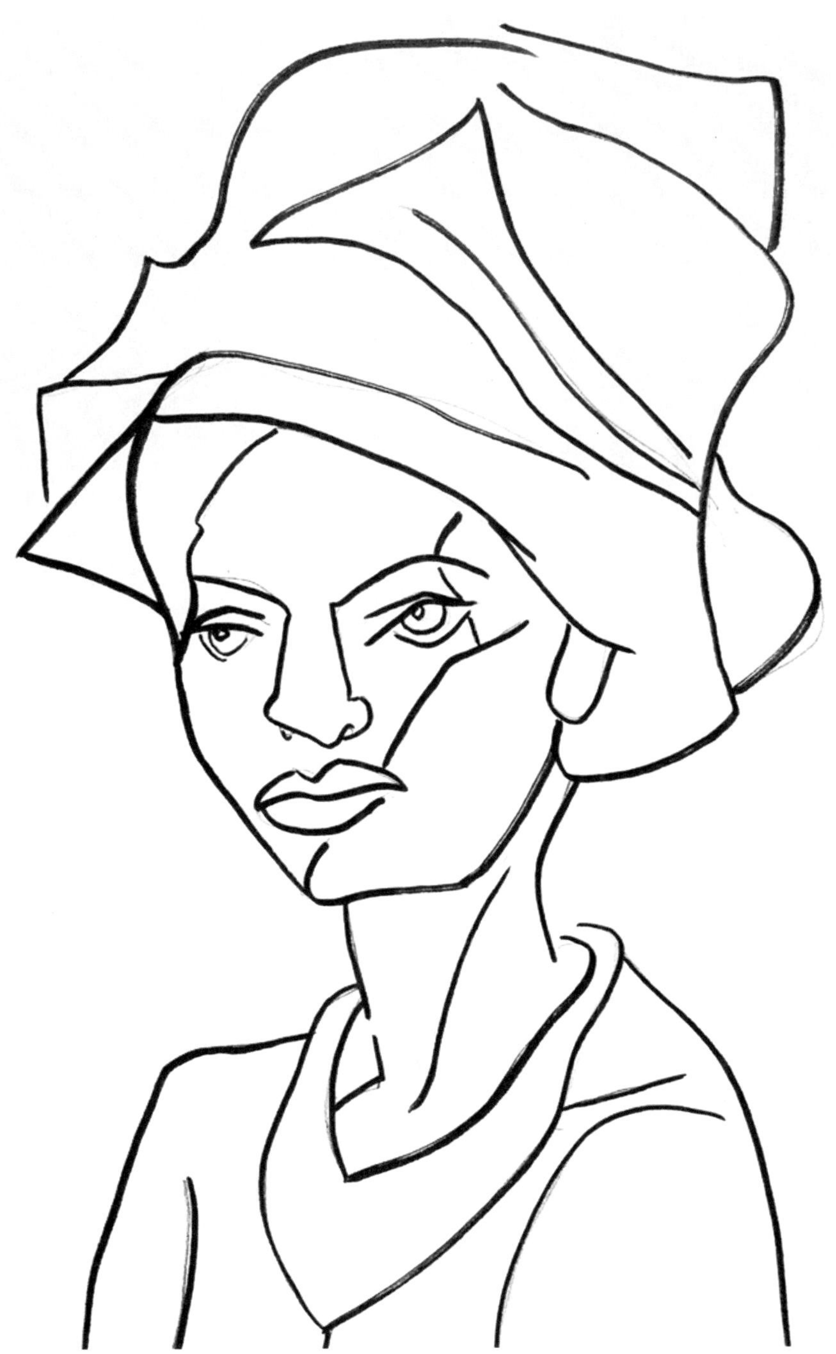

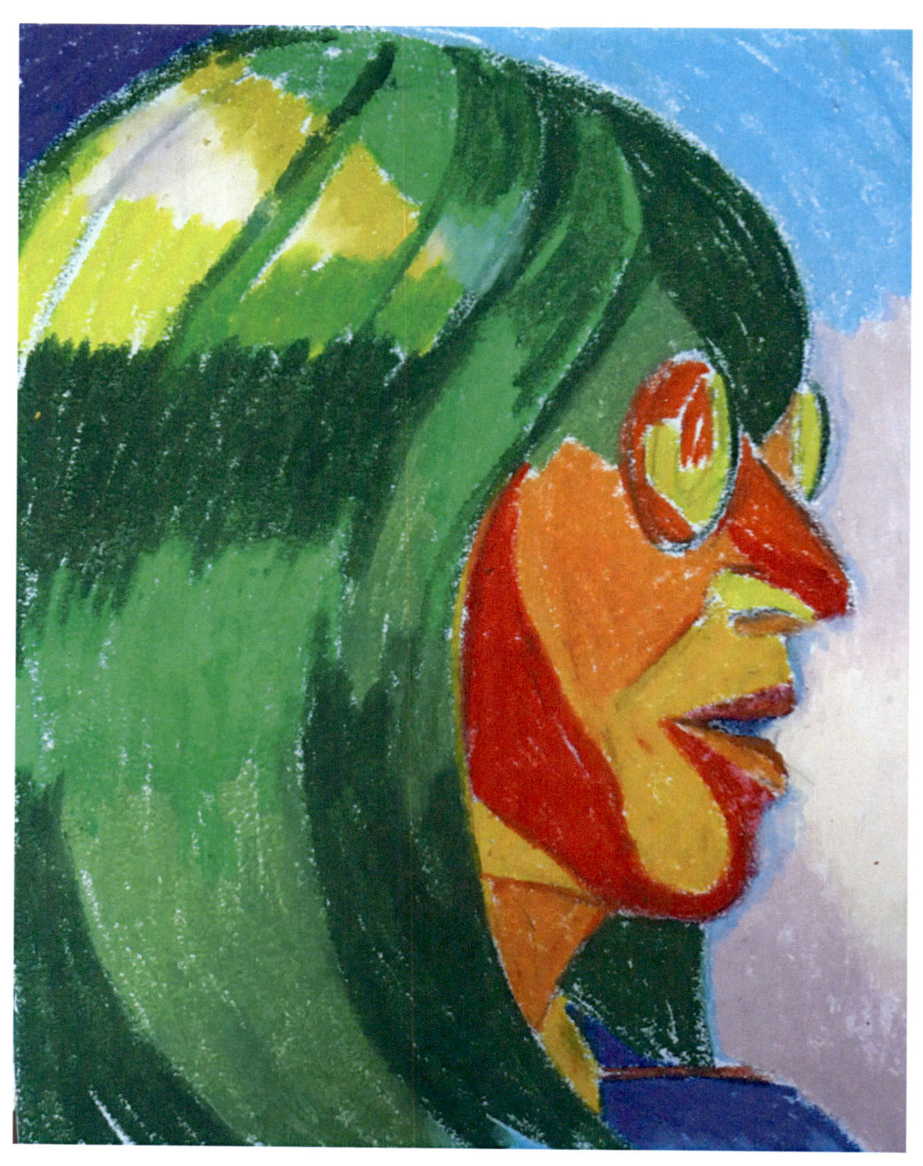

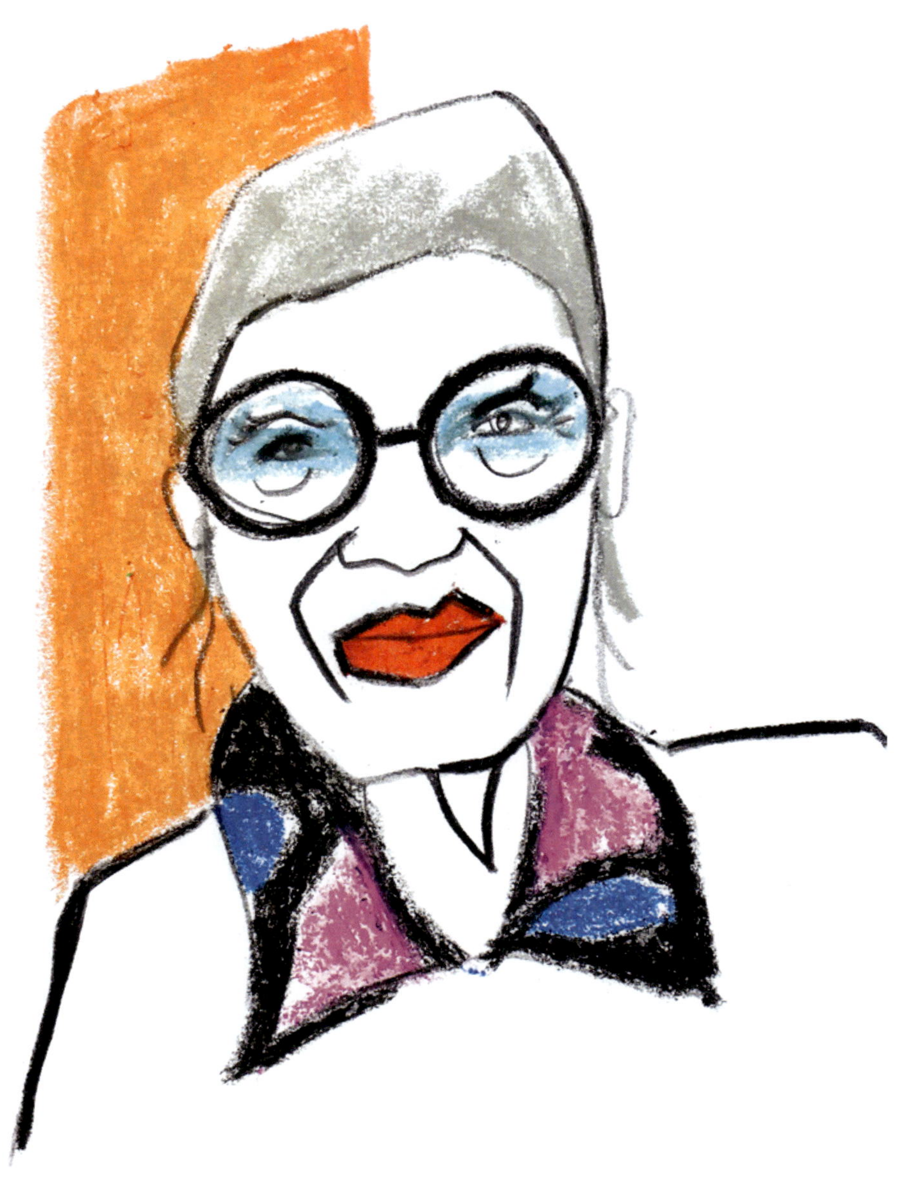

A Drawing a Day

Stella Downing

At the start of Lockdown, time suddenly seemed to slow down without the normal distractions, and I felt cut adrift from my family and friends. My husband and daughter both work for the NHS, my mother is 90 years old and lives alone, and our youngest daughter and her husband had their first baby, who was just two weeks old at the start of Lockdown. Our family are very close and I missed them all very much.

I decided to do a drawing every day on my daily walk in the woods near our house. I felt so grateful to be able to walk amongst the trees. I wrote titles and dates on my Moleskine concertina sketch books and decided that rather than being self critical of my work, I would simply draw or paint every day and the creative act would be the focus. Drawing created a structure to my day and I found it became a calm and meditative process where I could forget all my anxieties for a short while. There was a sense of freedom in having all this time and not being bound by normal daily routines.

Drawing and being amongst nature helped keep me centred. I would go into the woods every day, whatever the weather was like: rain, wind, sunshine, and make drawings. In warm weather I would stay as long as I could, sometimes two or three hours, observing the changing state of the trees, the gradual unfurling of leaves and flowers, first the bluebells, then the wild garlic, then the Nottingham Lace.

The certainty of the changing seasons and the absolute beauty of nature became the focus of calm each day. At times it felt almost dreamlike. I was aware of the intensity of colours and the beauty of birdsong and the feeling of safety cocooned amongst the trees.

I completed five little books in total, so this is a small selection of images from those concertina books and pastel paintings. I am grateful that I have had this opportunity to slow down, to look and listen. I look back on this strange period of time now with a realisation of what's truly important to me.

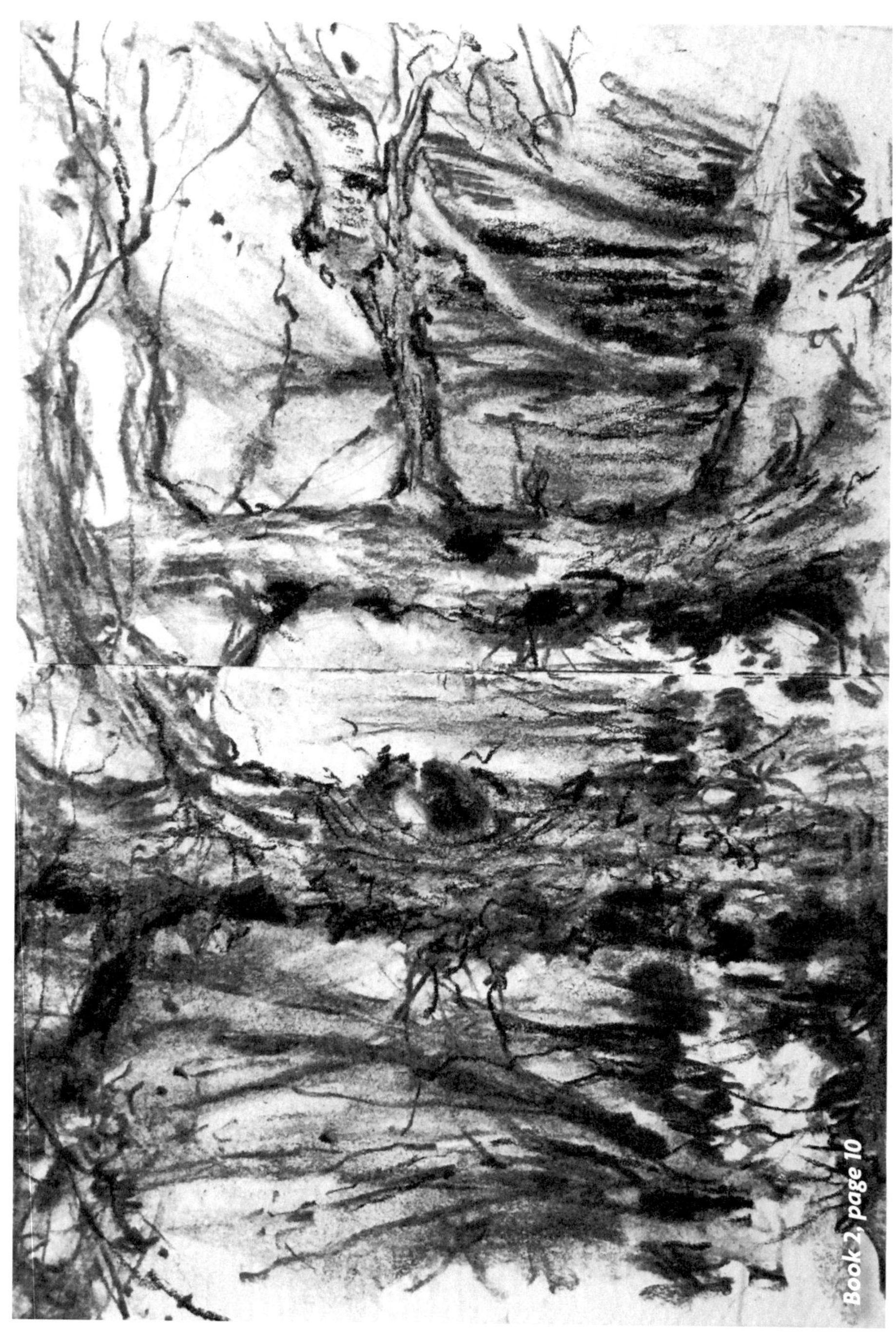

Book 2, page 10

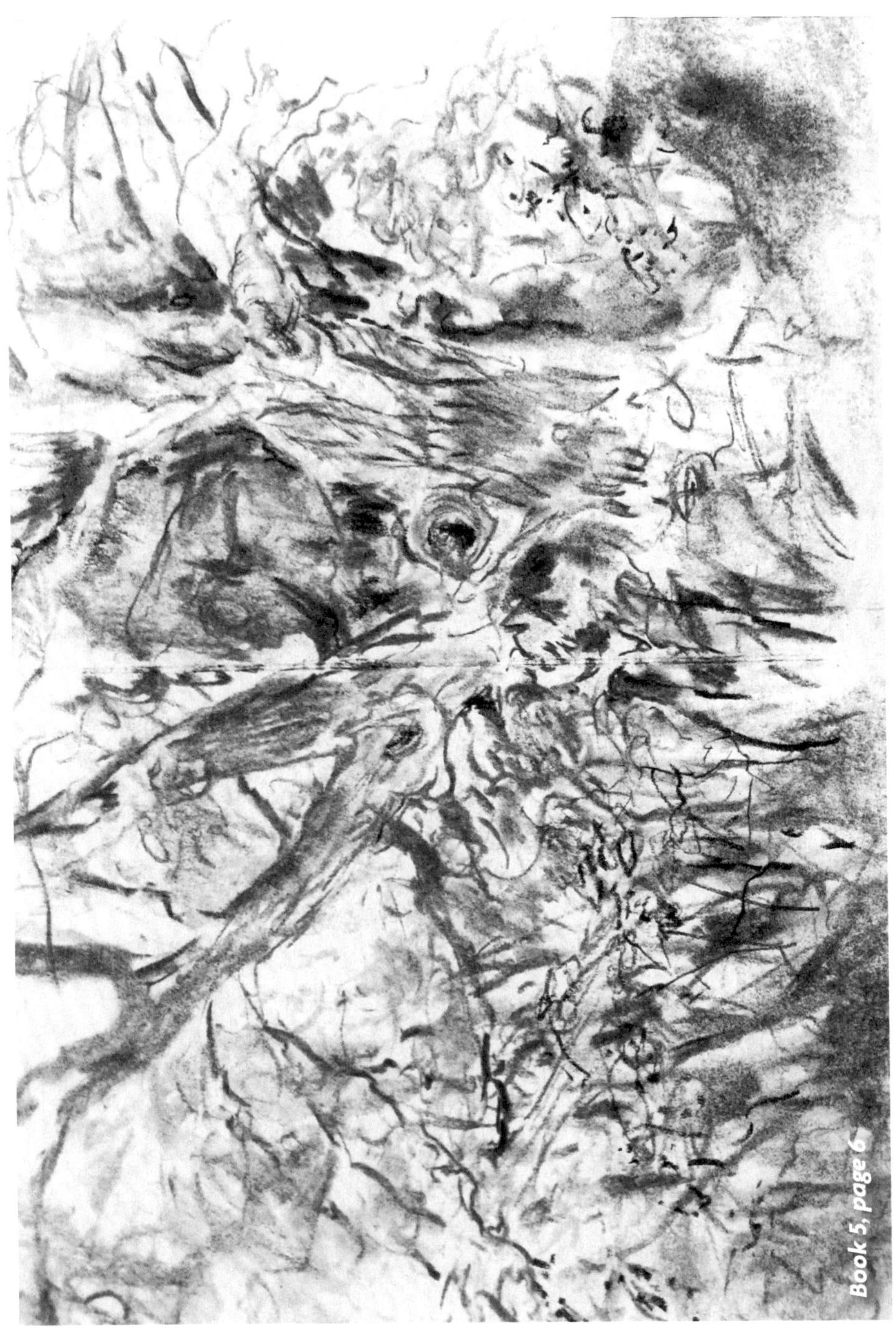

Book 5, page 6

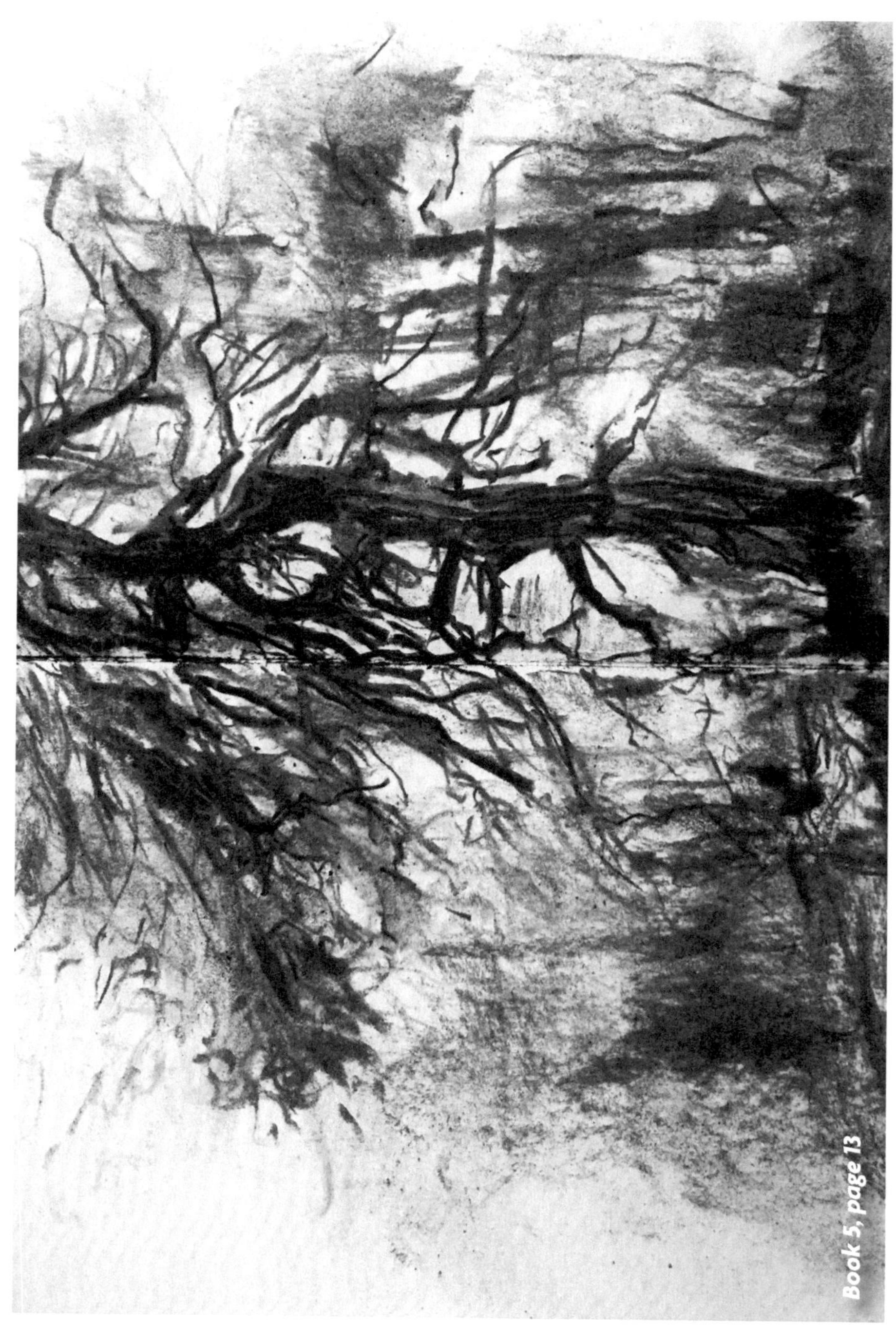
Book 5, page 13

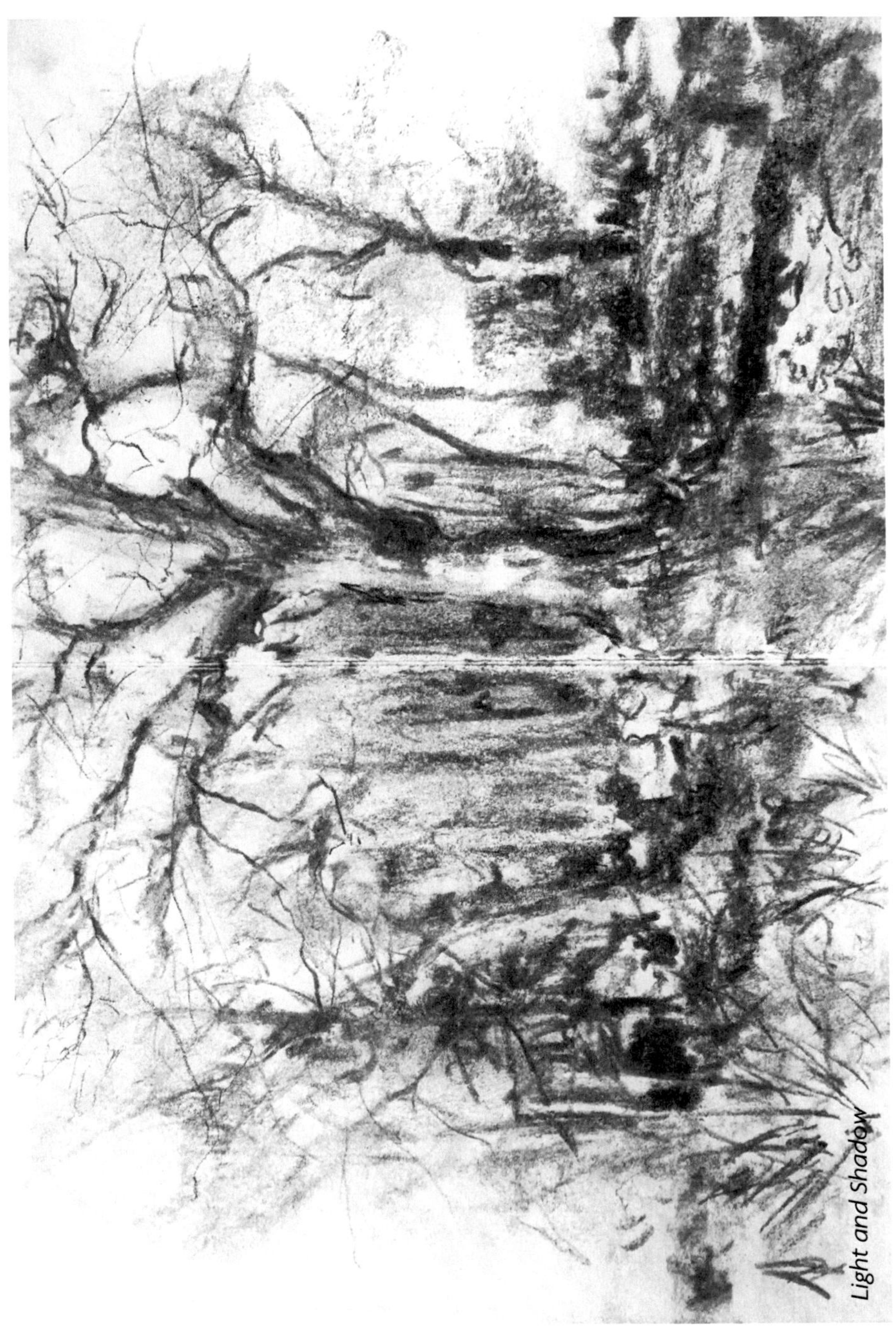

Light and Shadow

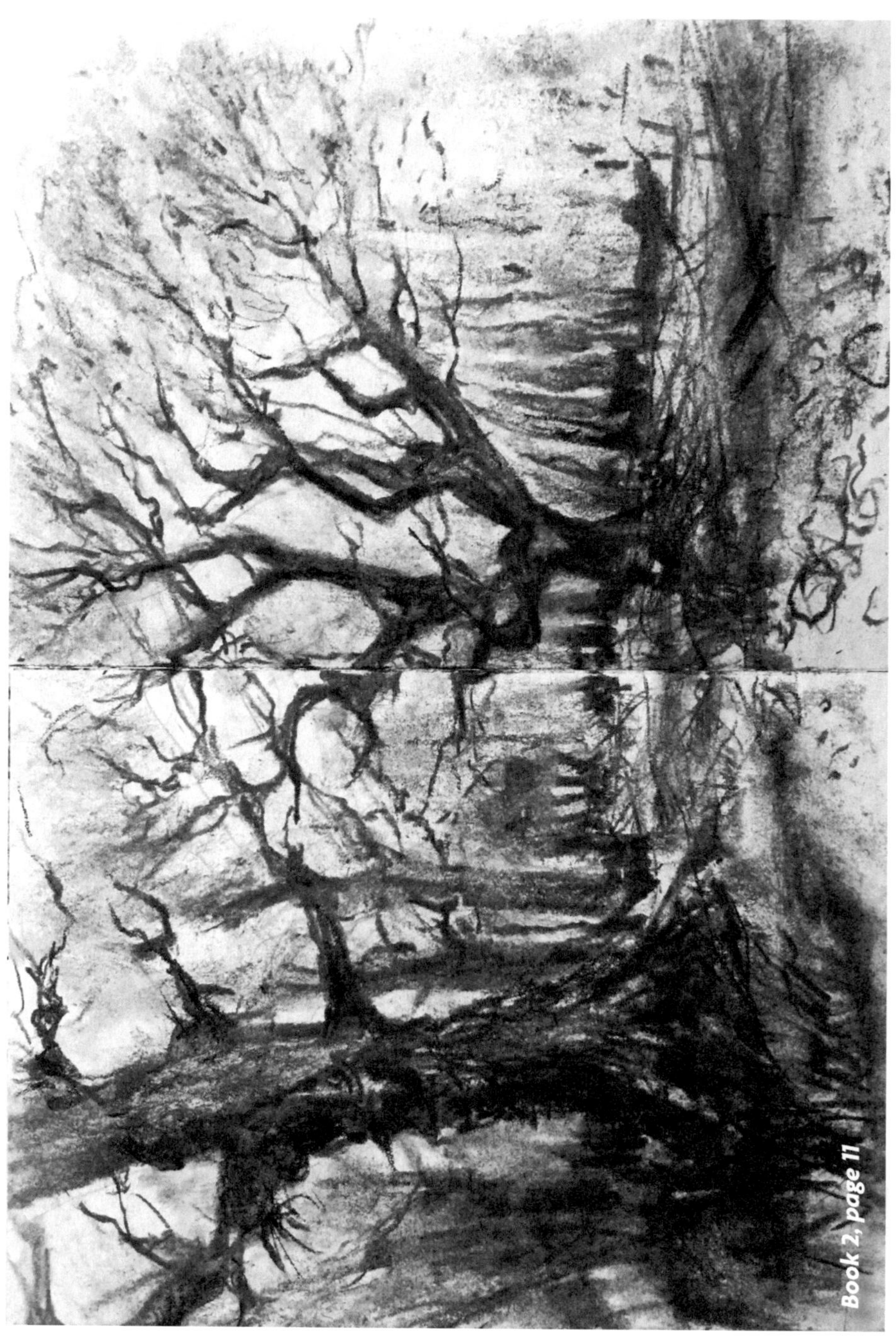
Book 2, page 11

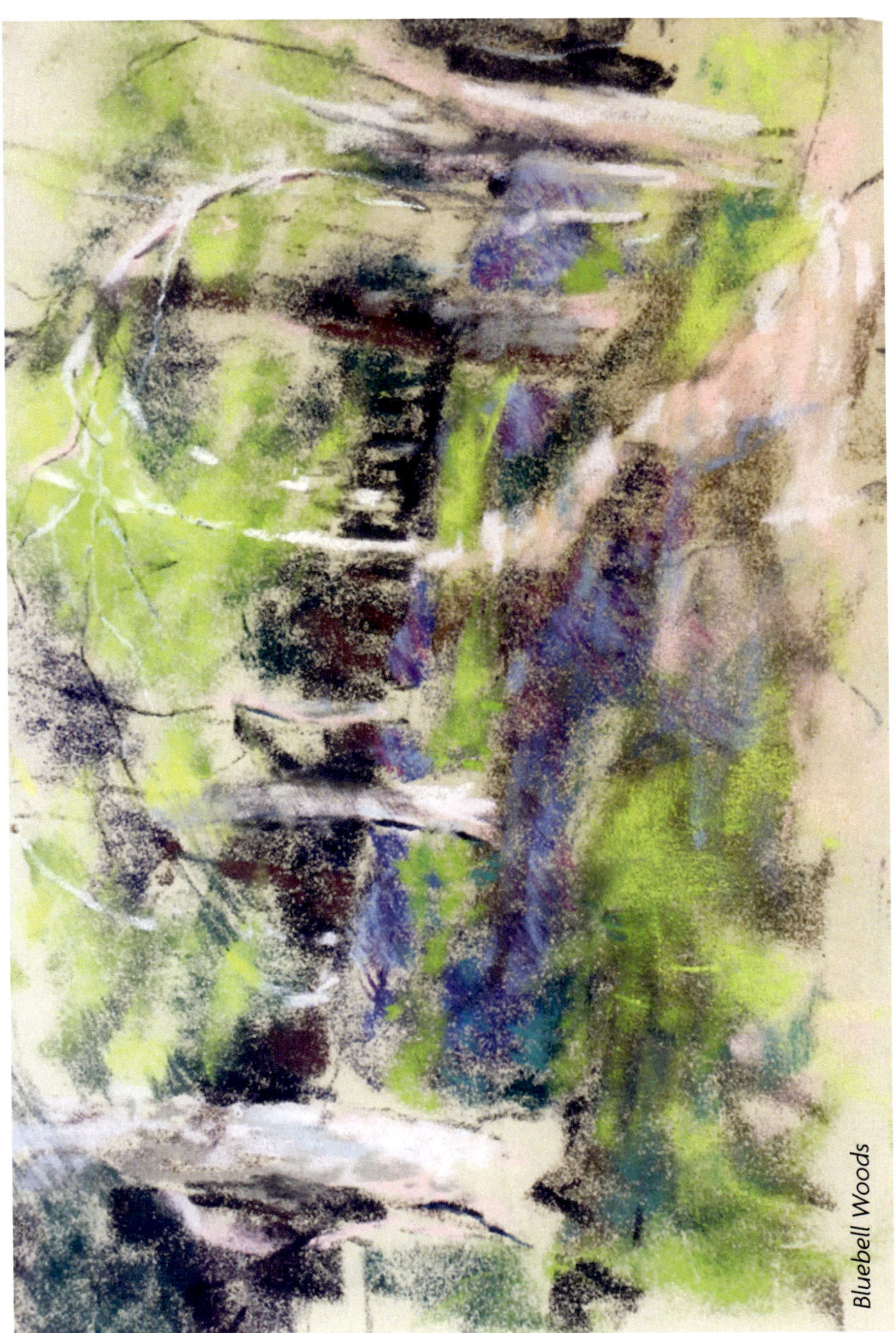

Bluebell Woods

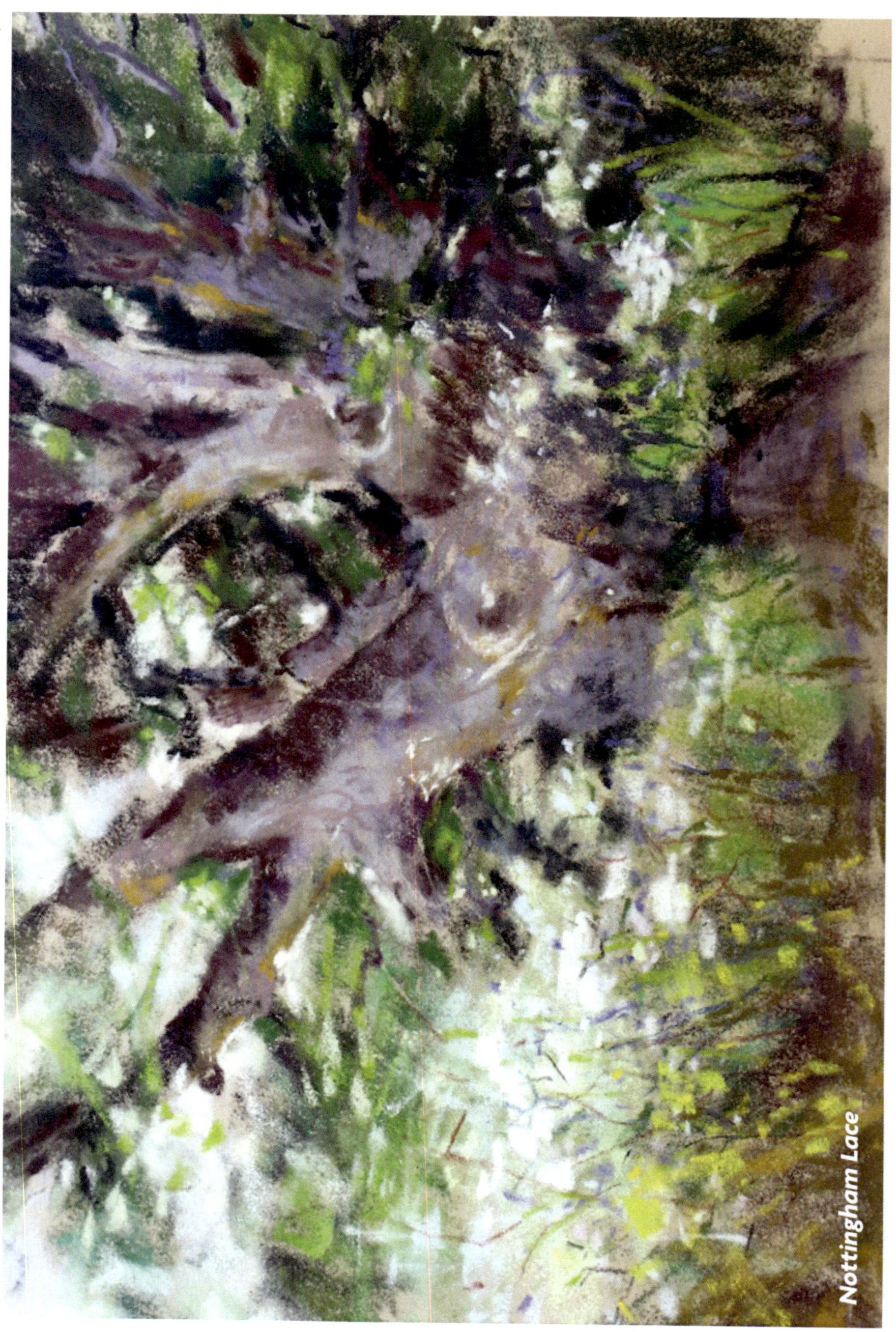

Nottingham Lace

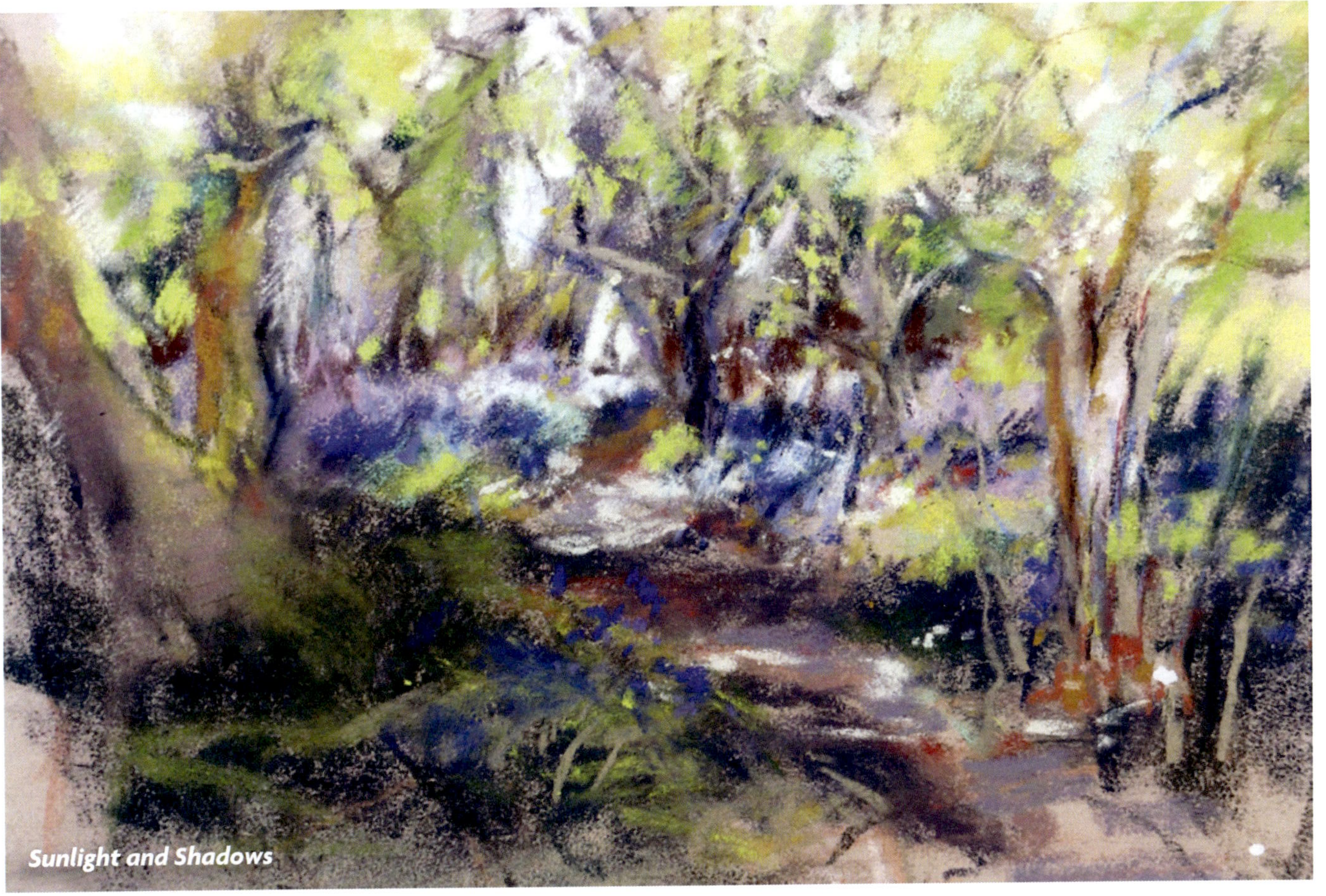

Sunlight and Shadows

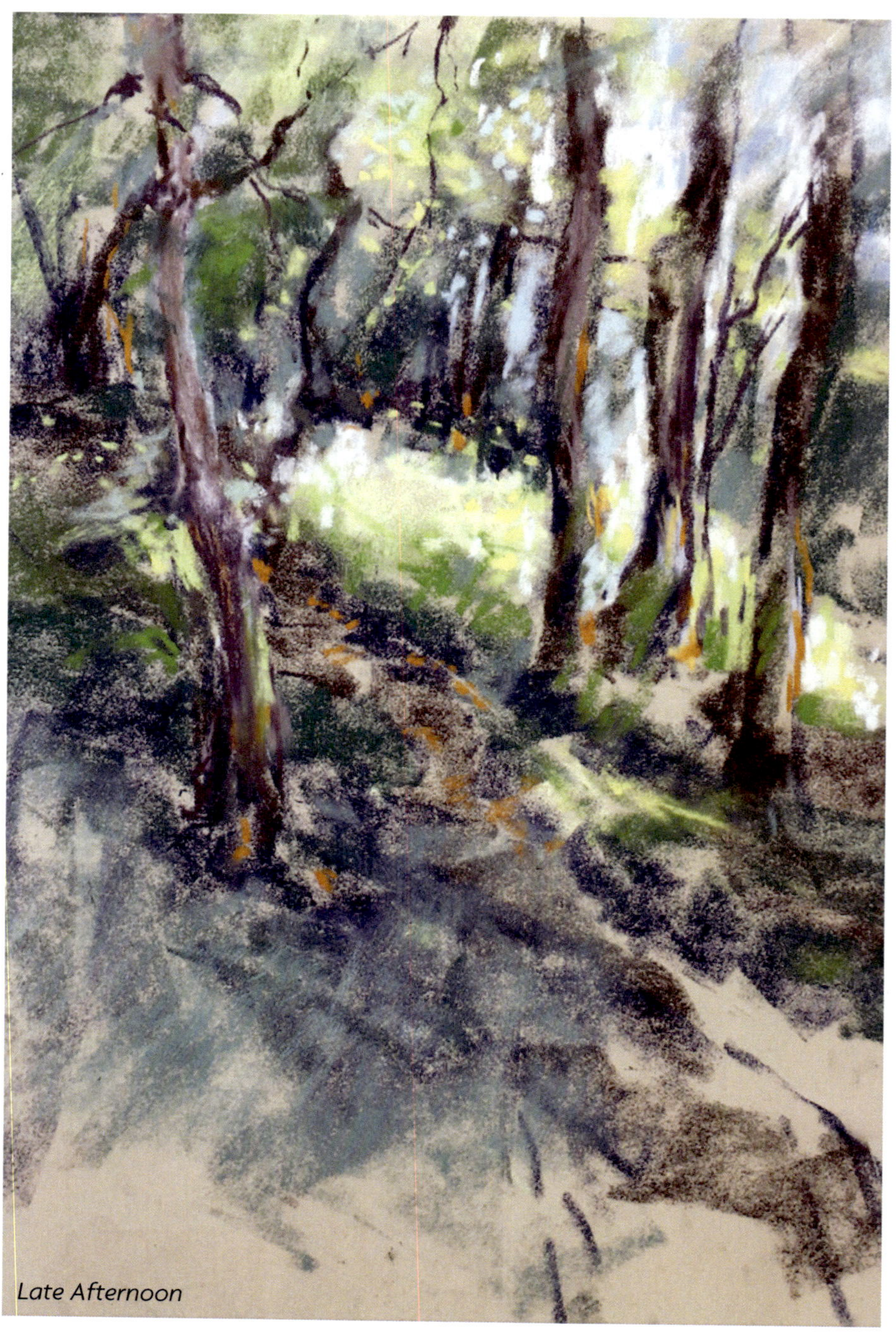

Late Afternoon

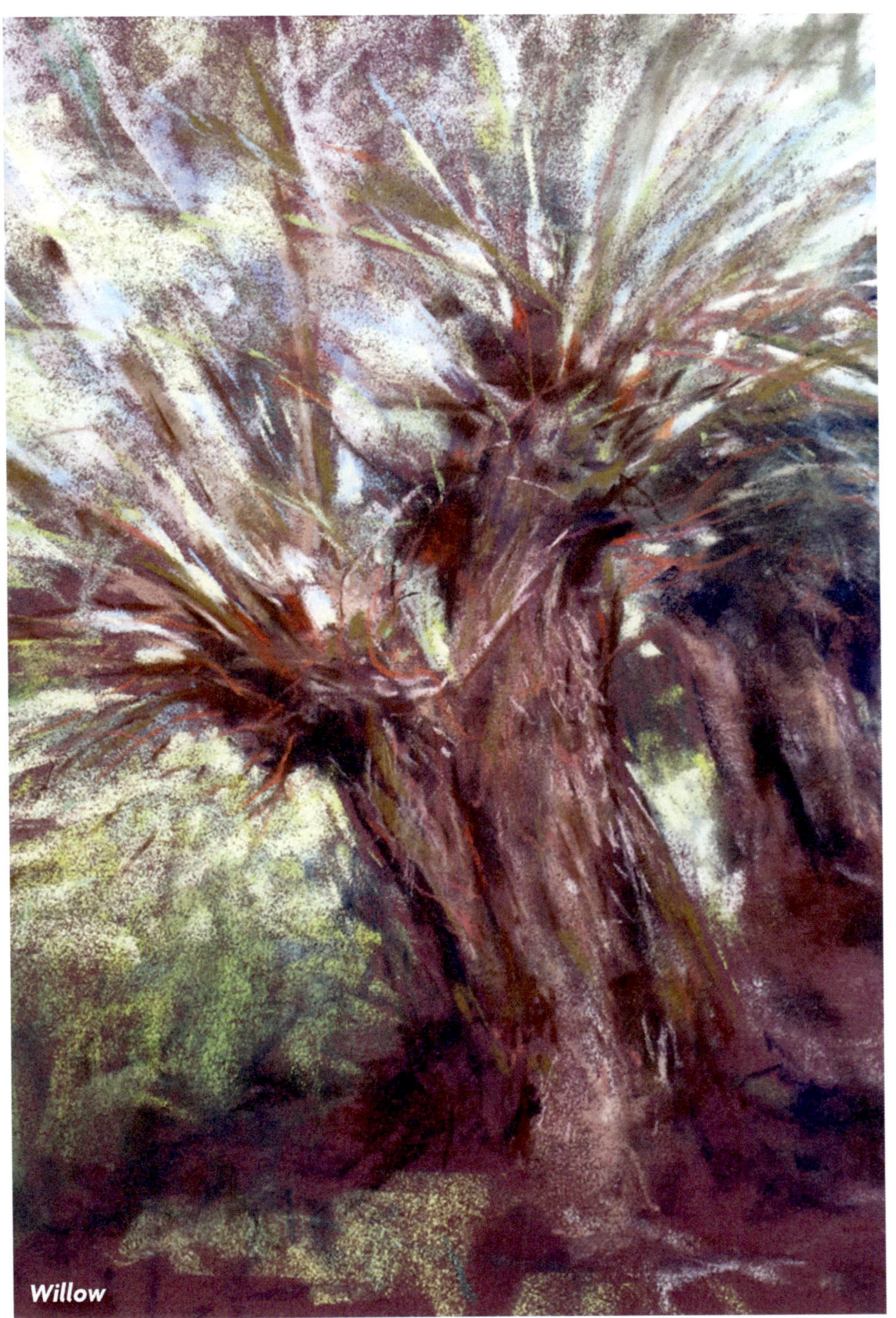
Willow

My Refuge

Sue Haslam

The announcement of lockdown came as a big shock, I hadn't thought it would come to that. Then there was talk of things we could do to benefit from the enforced time at home, but I couldn't concentrate on anything except cleaning, clearing out and gardening to begin with. A new routine was underlined by bad news and scary statistics announced each day in the Downing Street briefings, and they kept getting worse. So we had to look for the positives. I was healthy, and my family and friends were healthy. I slept well - no deadlines to meet, no events to prepare for, few decisions to make - though I had those vivid, weird dreams too. For me, the good weather was the saving grace - it meant we could enjoy our daily exercise outdoors, we could garden, and some of our shopping for essentials could be done by bicycle.

After a couple of weeks, I missed my usual art outings. I thought 'I've got to get creative at home instead', and turned half of my shed into a studio. One sunny afternoon, I drew the pollarded sycamore that was sprouting new leaves. After a hot morning's gardening, I drew the vegetable plot. Reclining on the deckchair, I drew the Worcester Pearmain in the spring sunshine. And so it went on. Painting and drawing was immersive, it was a welcome respite from all the bad, sad stuff going on in the world outside. My sunny garden was a refuge, a place of peace and safety, and recording different views of it became an expression of gratitude.

Along with the NHS rainbows, someone had the idea of placing teddy bears in windows, so that children could make their daily walk into a 'bear hunt'. In our tiny village that wasn't going to work, but 'guerrilla art' appeals to me, so evening bike rides became a mission to graffiti teddies discretely onto walls, poles and posts. For Easter Sunday, I stencilled three yellow chicks on the old black barn. The ongoing project is painting bears, suns, and rainbows onto pebbles and leaving them to be found by whoever.

I gardened, read books, exchanged letters with friends, and kept a brief diary, but drawing and painting were my creative responses to the pandemic and lockdown. These aren't the only unpleasant times when art has come to my rescue, and I don't suppose they'll be the last...

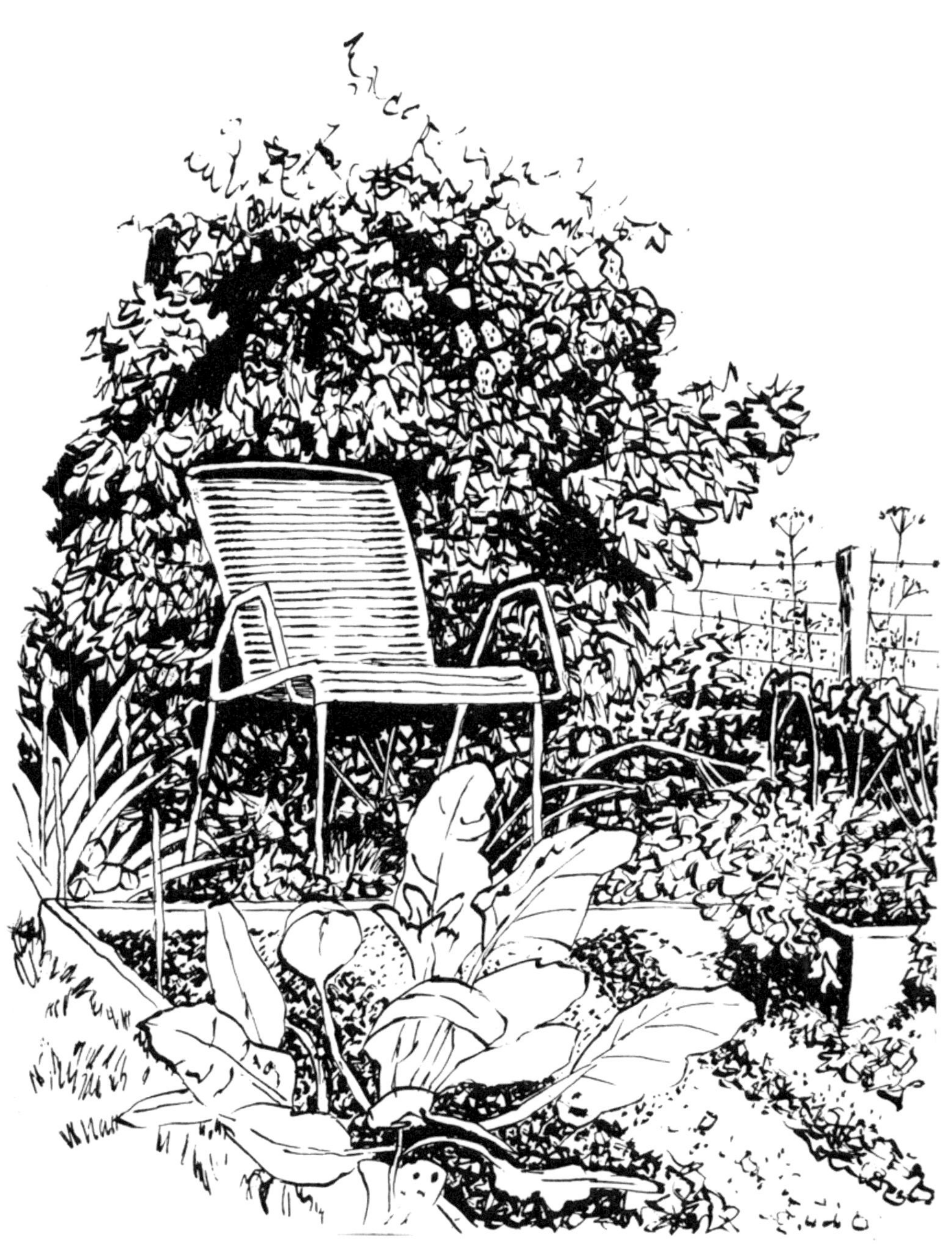

The vegetable patch

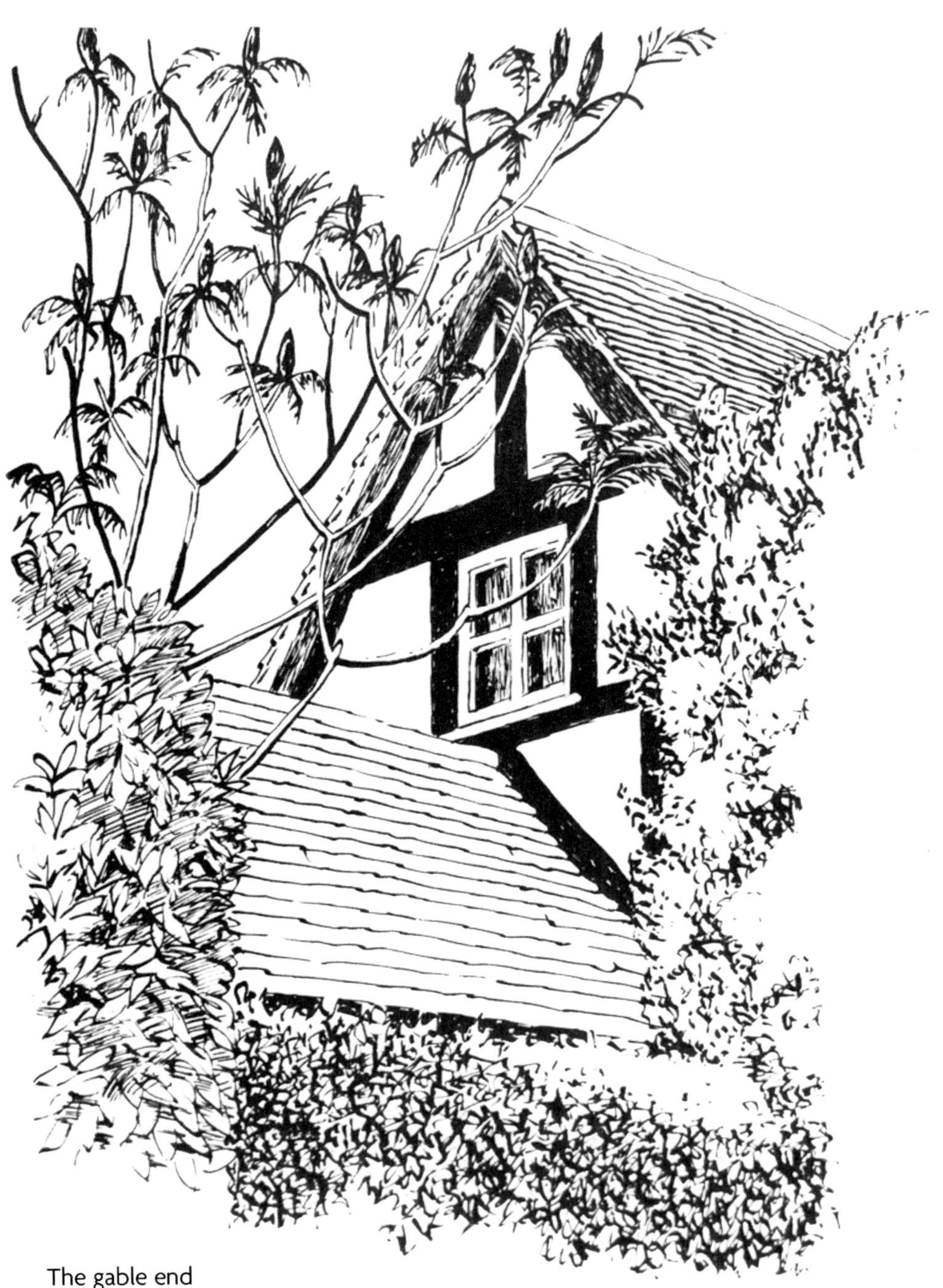

The gable end

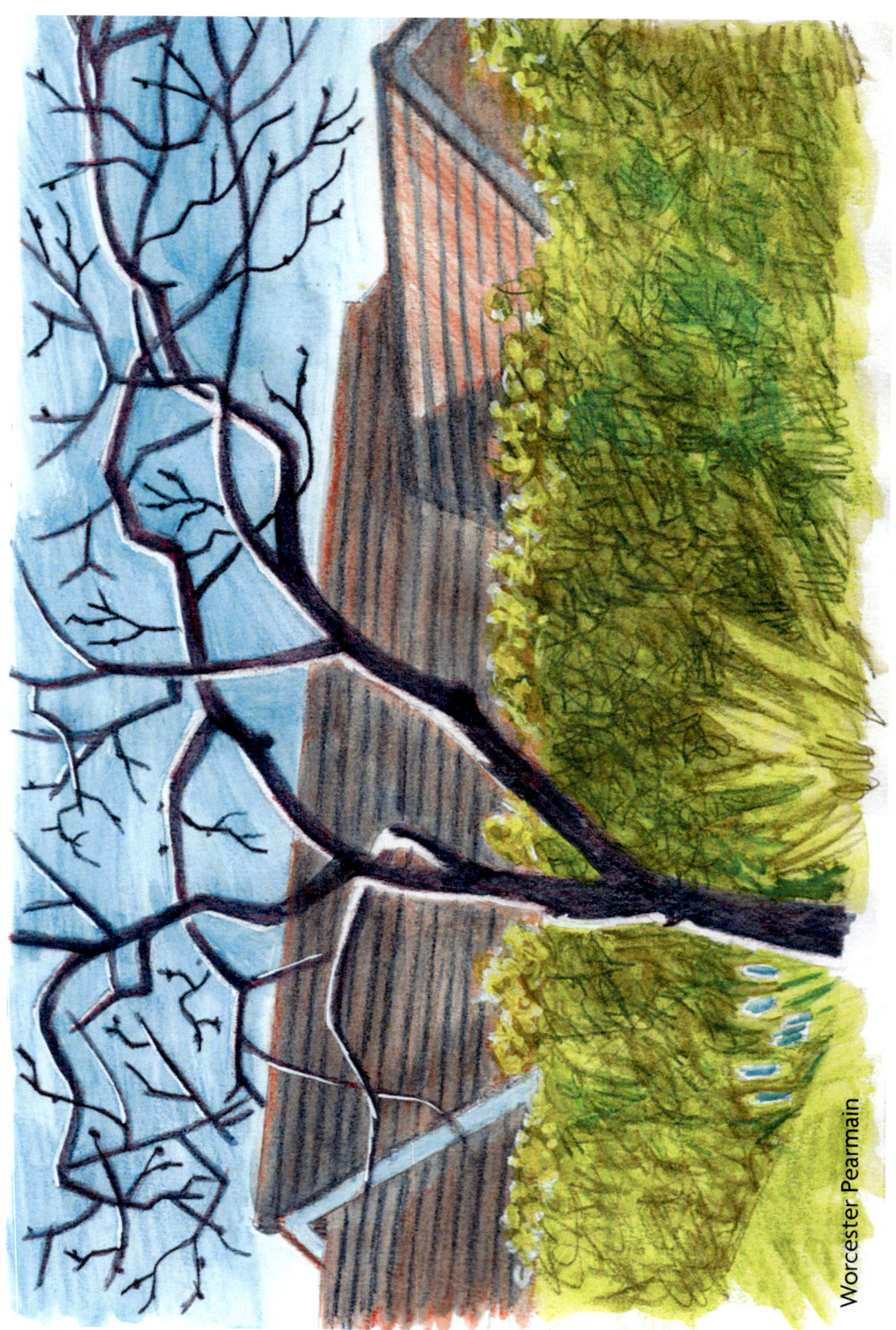

Worcester Pearmain

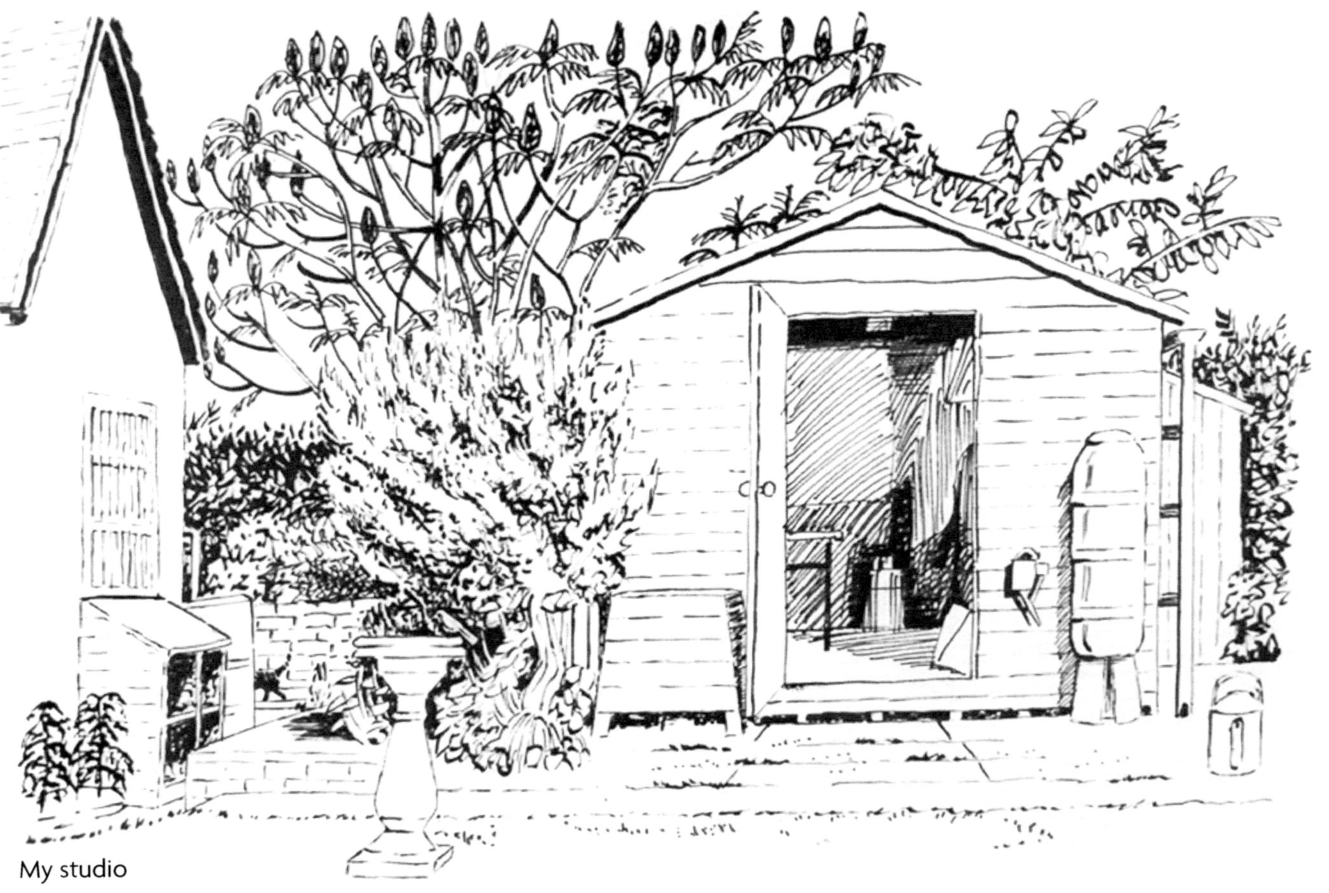

My studio

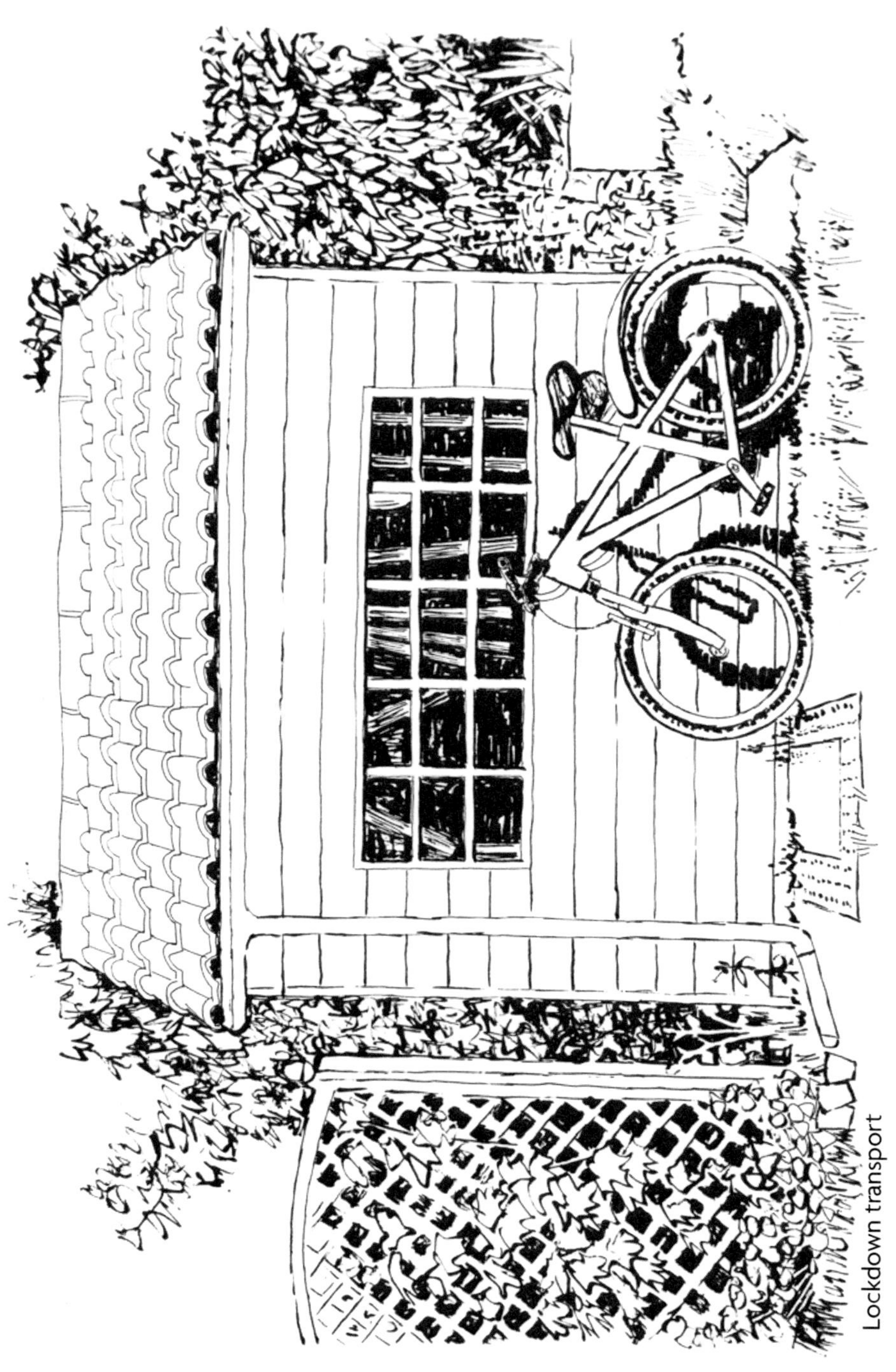

Lockdown transport

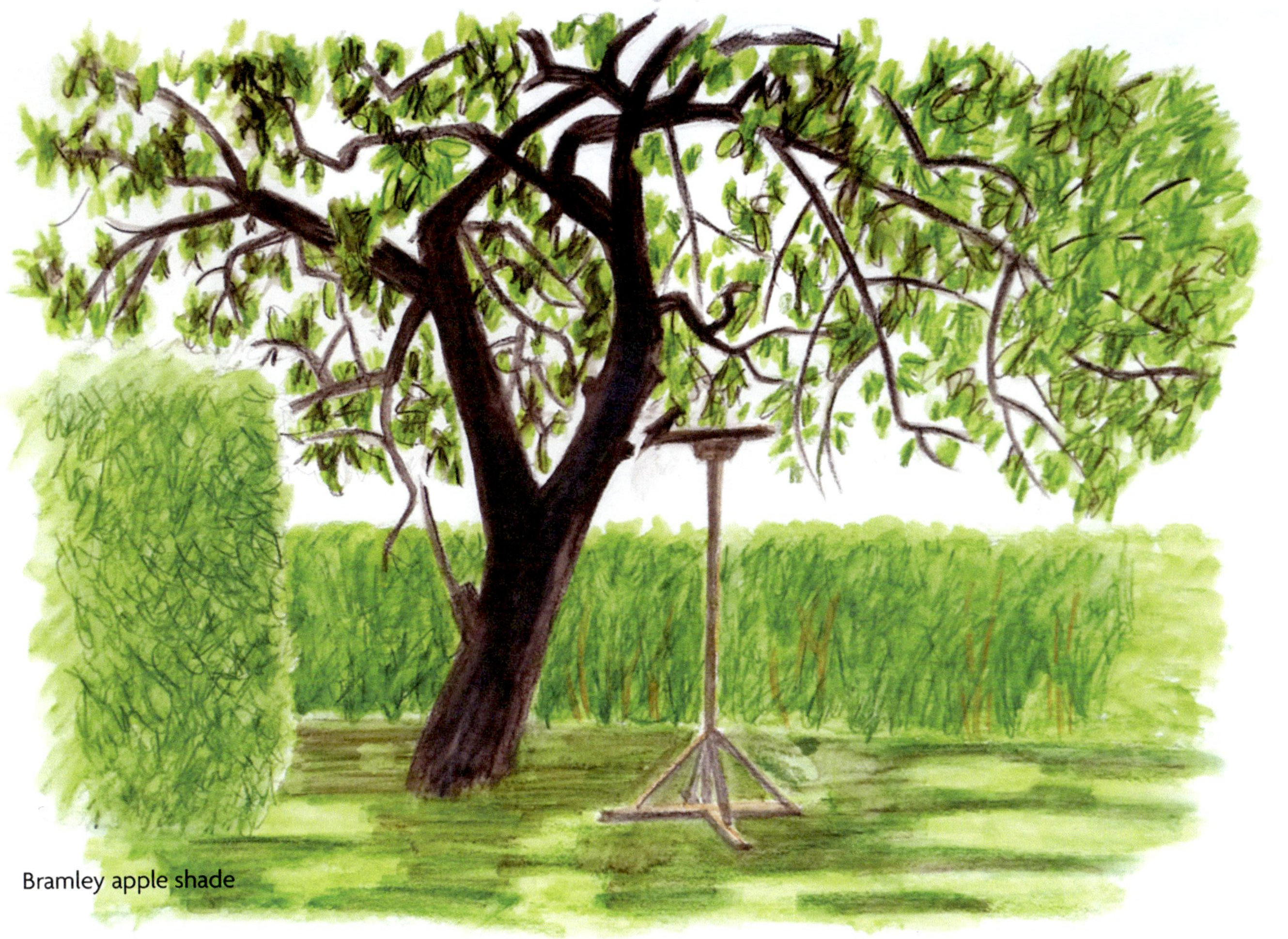

Bramley apple shade

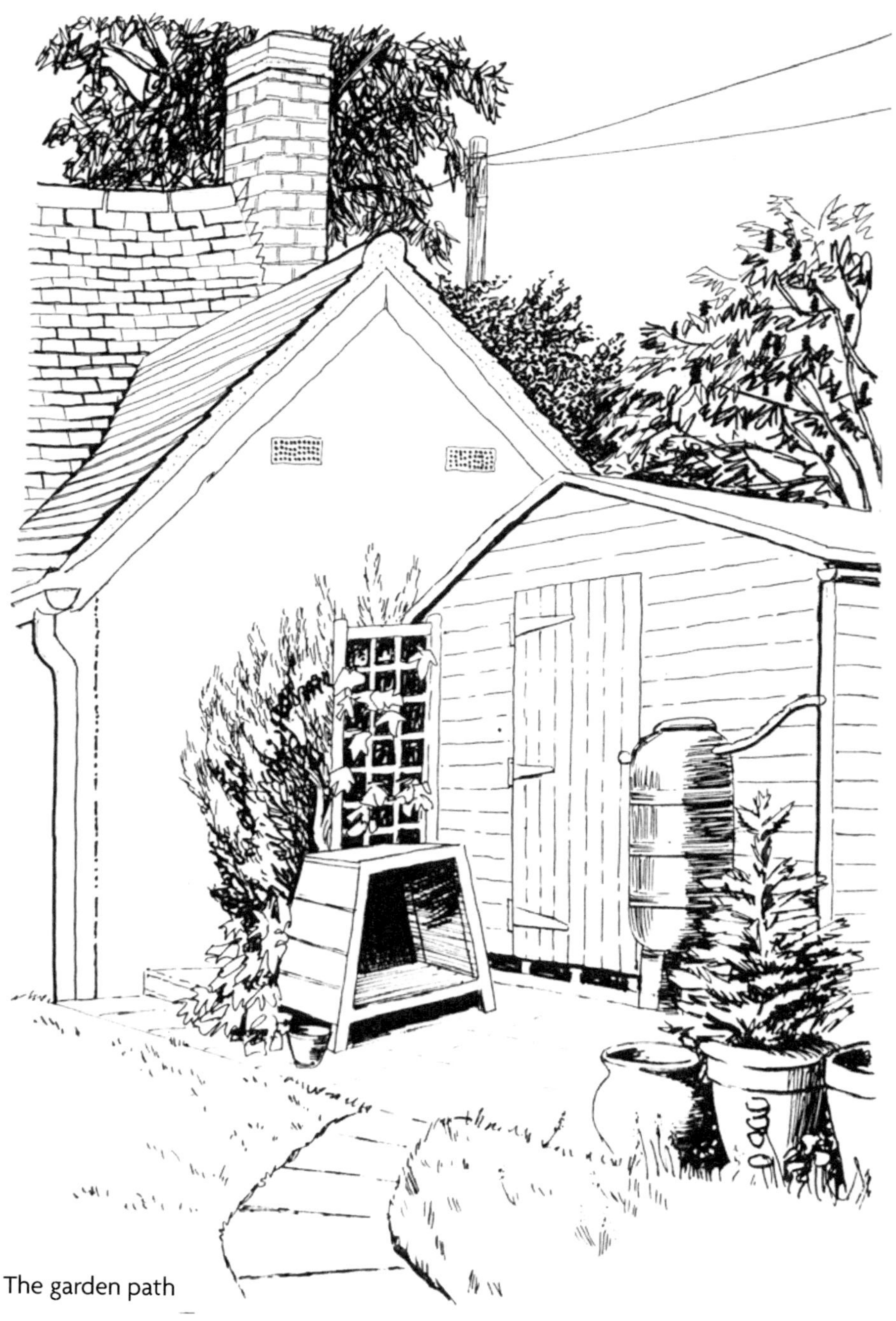

The garden path

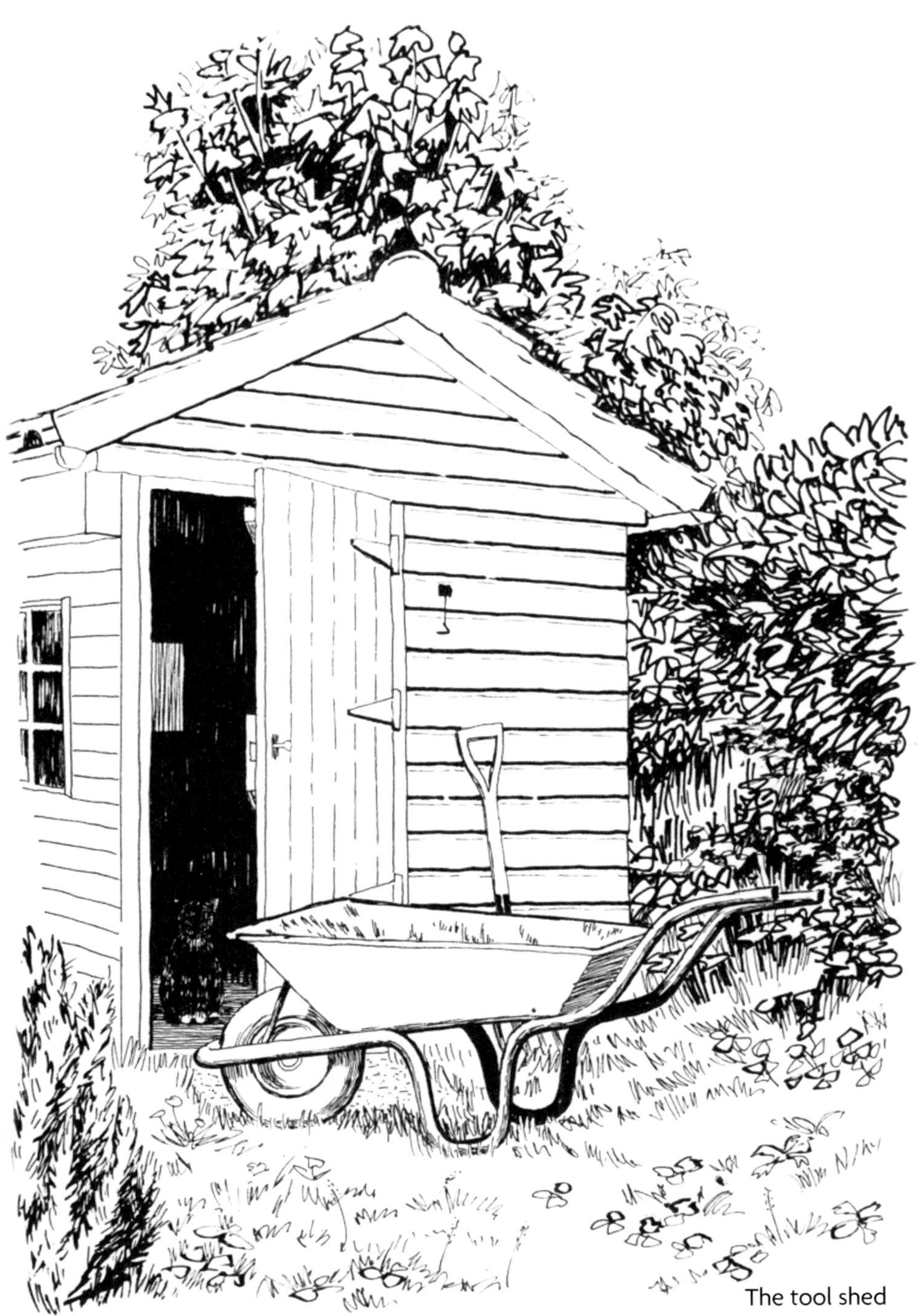
The tool shed

A Bear Hunt

I don't know if anyone 'hunted' these graffiti bears in our village, but it amused me to gradually increase their number to 19 by the Easter weekend.

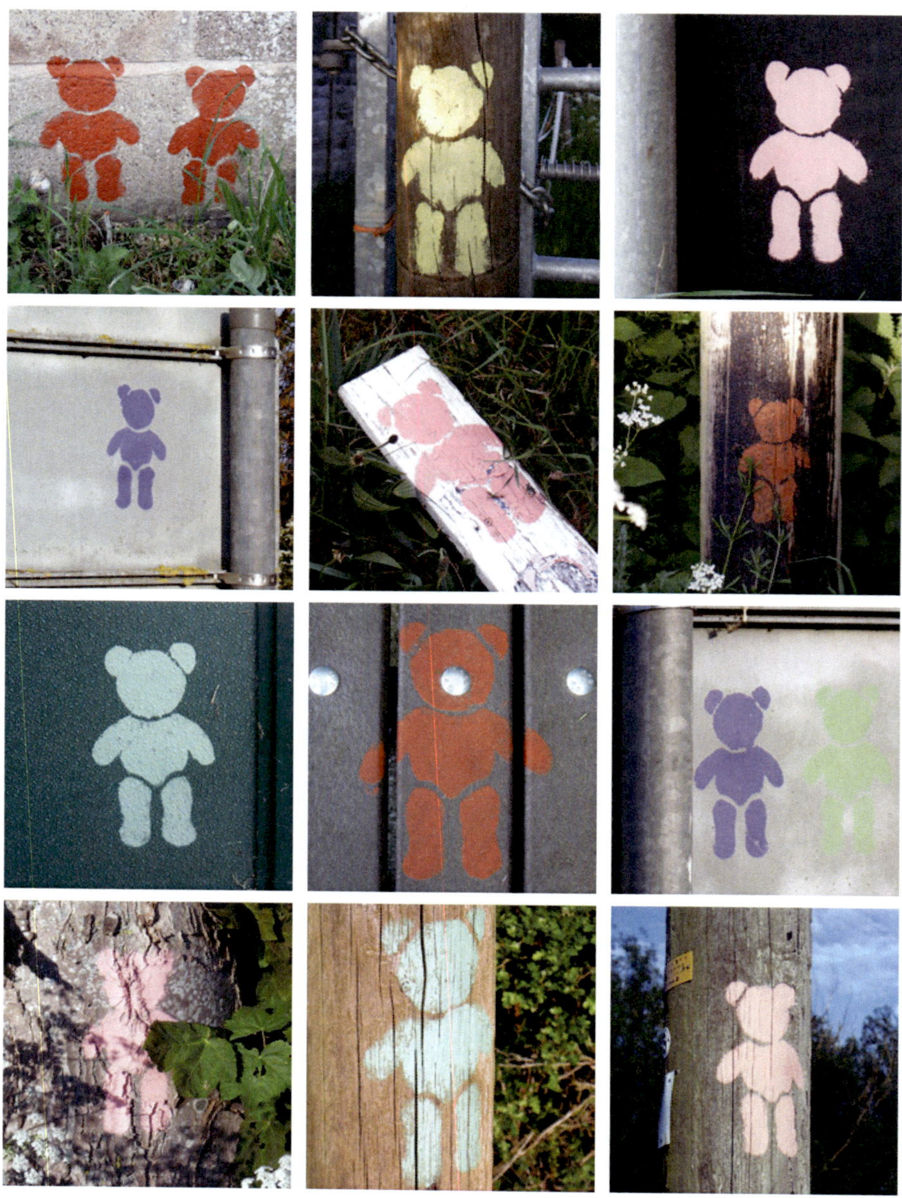

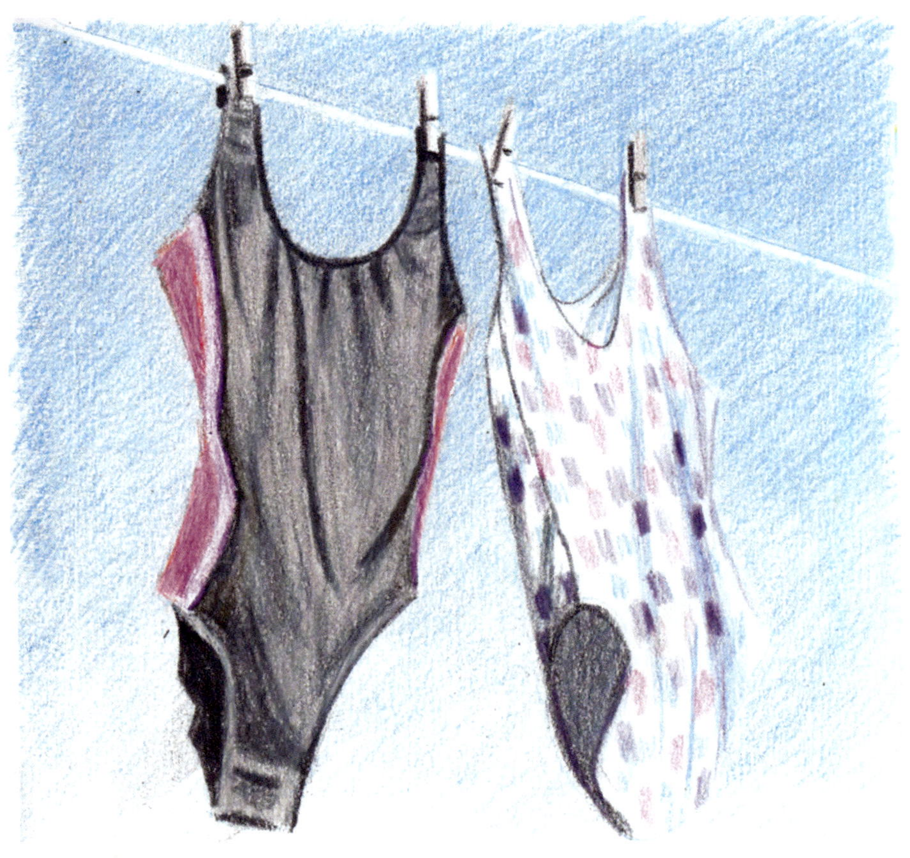

Things I won't be needing for a while...

I love swimming: lane swims and aqua aerobics have been especially important forms of exercise since I developed arthritis in one knee. My last visit to the pool before lockdown was on March 20th.

My freshly-washed swimsuits hung on the line on Monday 23rd as a sad reminder of all the things we wouldn't be able to do for the foreseeable future.

10 x 10 Lockdown is the result of 10 women sharing 10 examples of their creative work, including making, drawing, painting and writing, between March and June 2020.

Weird times during which the women used their newly found space in individual ways...

All profits from the sale of this book will go to Women's Aid to support the victims of domestic abuse in lockdown and at all other times.

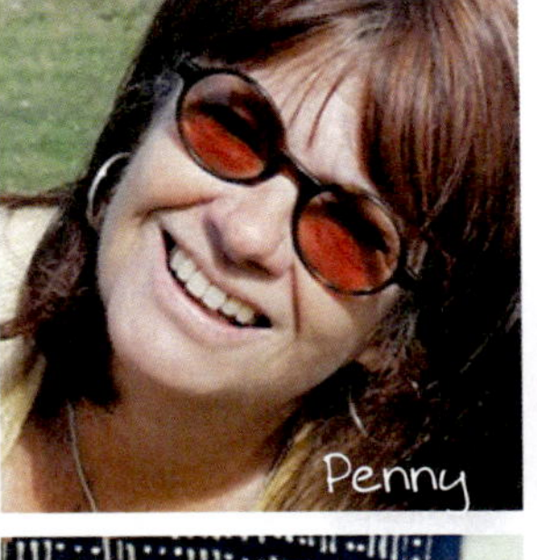
Penny

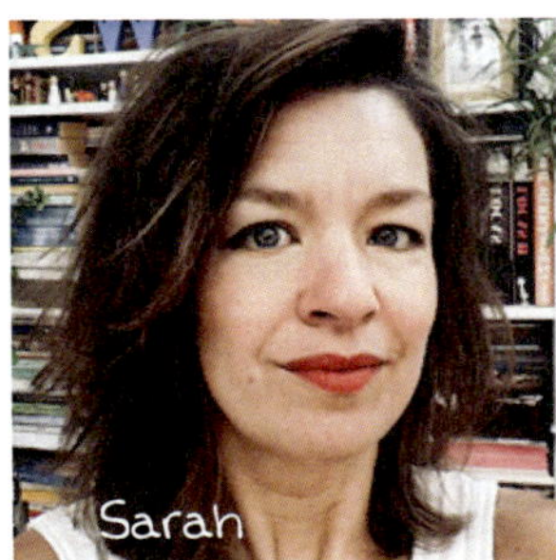
Sarah

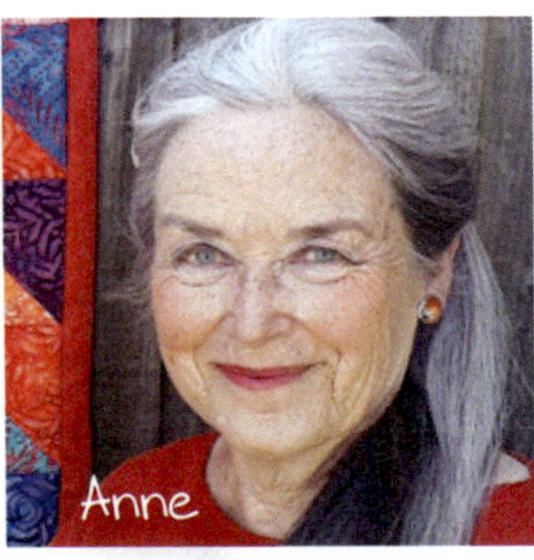
Anne

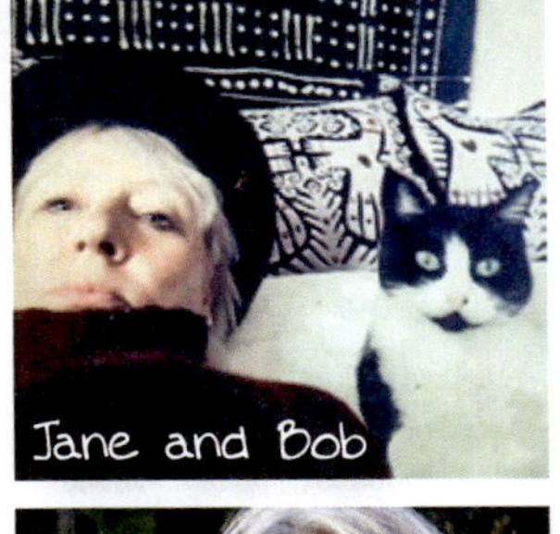
Jane and Bob

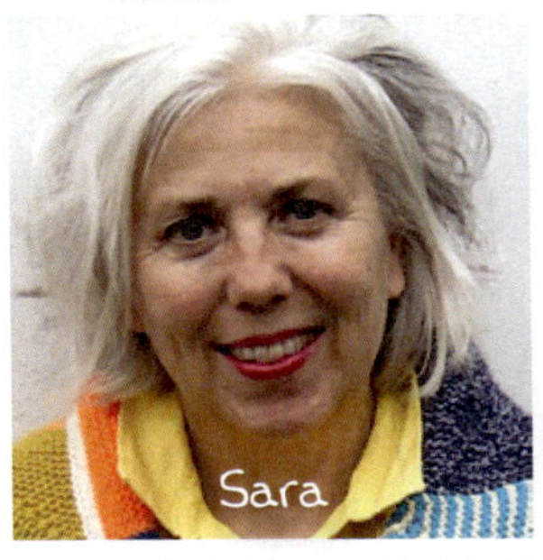
Sara

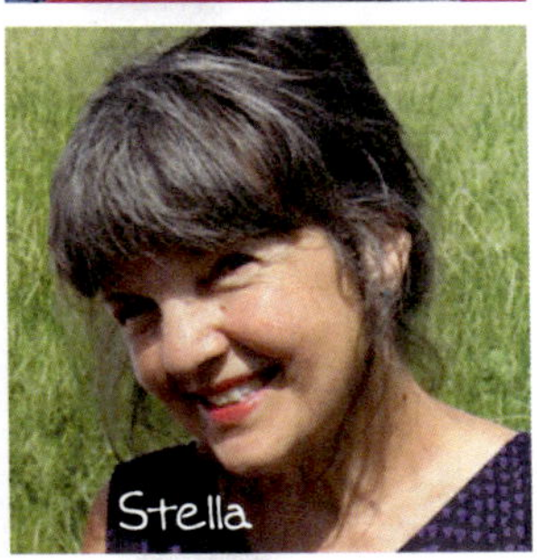
Stella

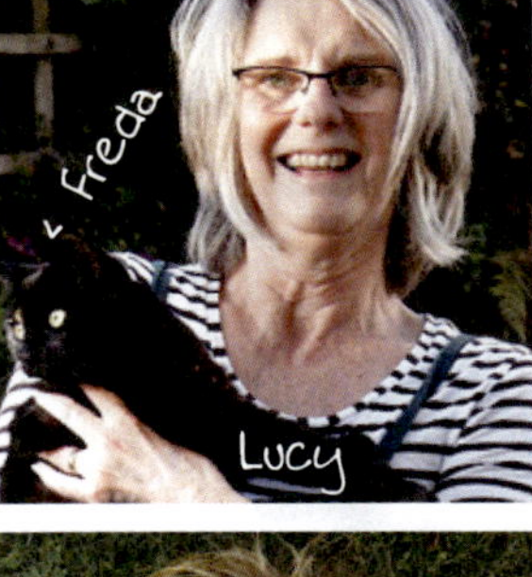
Freda
Lucy

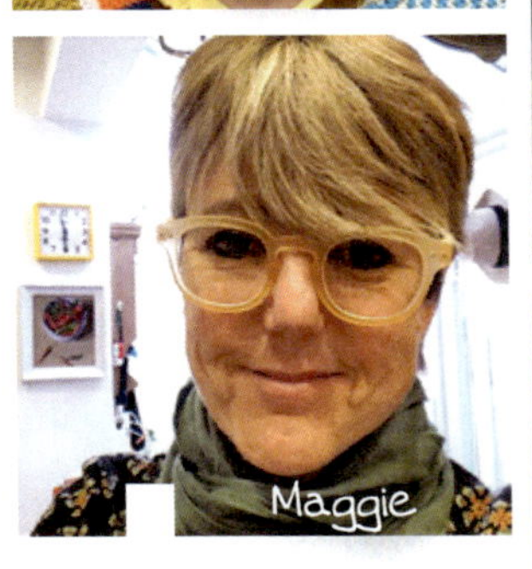
Maggie

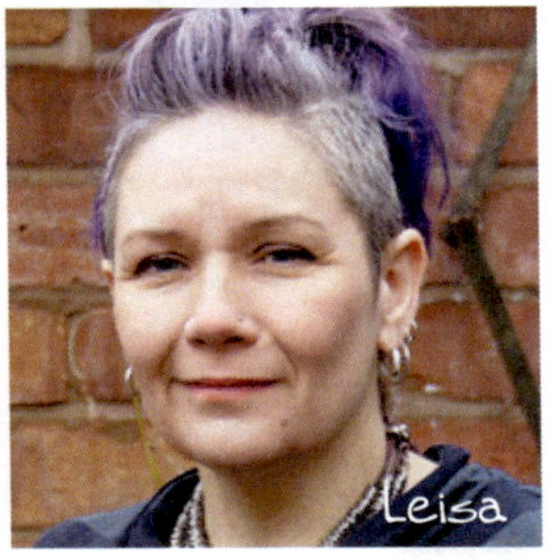
Leisa

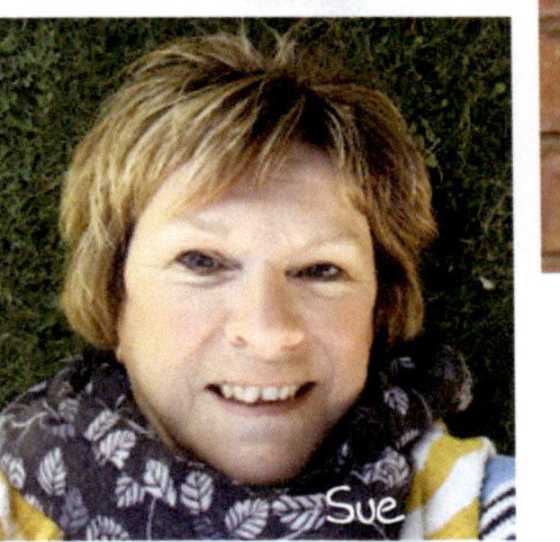
Sue

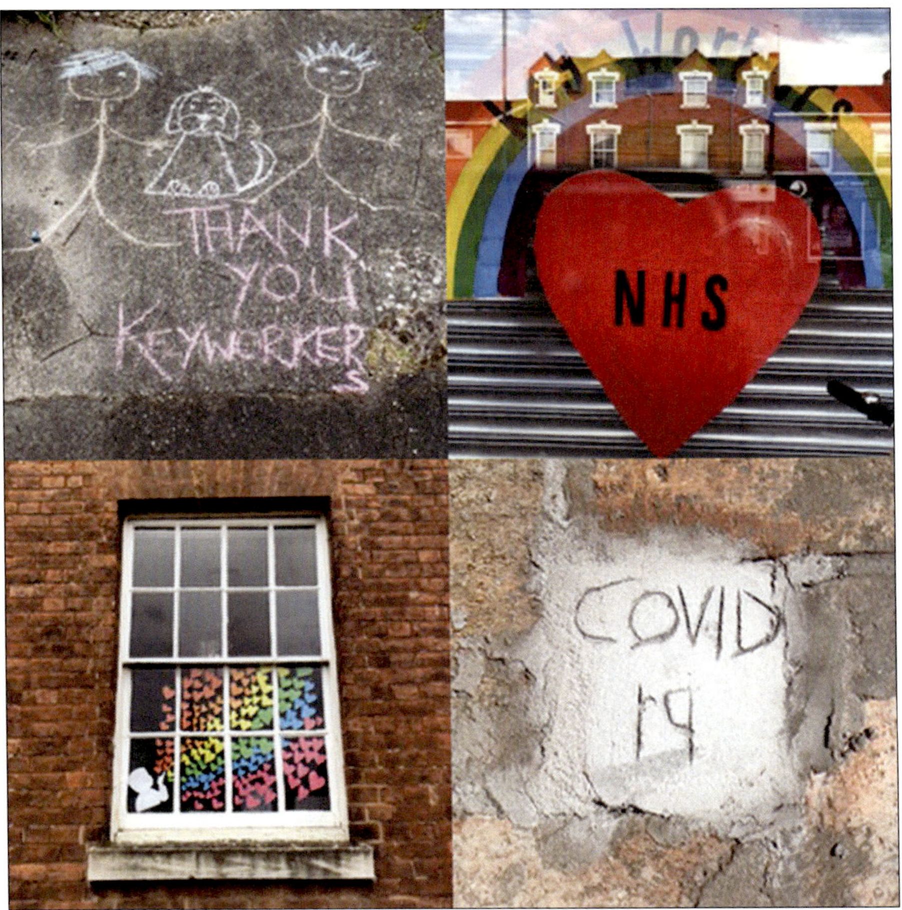

Over and Out *Maggie Keeble*

Thanks to

Fran Collingham for advertising and promotion
The estate of James Erlichman for initial funding of the project